Contemporary Machine-Embroidered Fashions

Transform Everyday Garments into Designer Originals

Eileen Roche

Published by

krause publications
An Imprint of F+W Publications

700 East State Street • Iola, WI 54990-0001
715-445-2214 • 888-457-2873

Library of Congress Catalog Number: 2006930838

ISBN-13: 978-0-89689-303-0
ISBN-10: 0-89689-303-0

Edited by Maria L. Turner and Andy Belmas
Designed by Marilyn McGrane
Illustrations by Deborah Peyton

Printed in the United States of America

Introduction

I know you. You have an embroidery machine (or want one very badly) and love embroidery. Naturally, you want to share your passion with others, and how best to do that than to showcase your embroidery on your clothing?

Many of you have followed embroidery trends through the pages of *Designs in Machine Embroidery* magazine. Since its inception in 1994, *Designs* has been on the cutting edge of the home embroidery industry. You have seen the changes in technology, technique and style. When I first learned to embroider, there was no education available—no magazines, no books, no classes, no events, no Web sites! Imagine how far we've come in a decade. I learned this craft the hard way—through trial and error, often in the wee hours of the morning. The good thing about that is I am just like you: a novice once and a student always.

This book shares many of the things I've learned along the way. From new techniques, time-saving tips and fashion-oriented details, you will benefit from my years of trial and error. I've broken down fashion embroidery into garment sections: pockets, collars, cuffs, necklines and open areas are the perfect place for embroidery embellishment. It's easier to attempt any large project when you break it down into smaller steps, which is the same with embroidery. Don't think about embroidery from neckline to hem; think about it in smaller sections. This approach also helps you define what looks best on you. Let's face it, one thing all embroidery has in common is the fact it draws attention to the garment. And not every figure needs that kind of scrutiny! Learn what flatters your figure and you'll never look at a blank garment the same again.

All of the designs shown in the book are included on the enclosed CD with the exception of the three monograms. You'll love the versatility of the embroidery designs—they were created specifically for you and your everyday wardrobe.

Contents

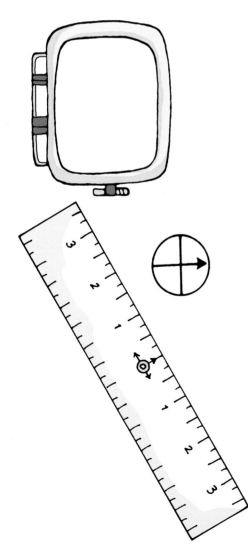

Chapter 1: Tips, Tricks and Techniques   6

Fashion Fundamentals for Machine Embroidery   8
- Using Blanks   8
- Dealing with Notions   11
- Designing the Embroidery Layout   11
- Letting the Garment Guide You   12
- Putting the Sketch into Reality   13

Embroidery Designs   14
- Preparing the Designs   14
- Organizing and Storing Your Designs   17

Templates: Your Road Map to Success   18
- What is a Template?   18
- How Do You Use Templates?   18
- Where Do You Get Templates?   19

Stabilizer   20
- Types of Stabilizers   21

Threads   22

Basic Hooping Techniques   23
- Setting Proper Hoop Tension   23
- Hooping   23

Helpful Tools   24
- Target Stickers   24
- Angle Finder   24
- Centering Rulers   25

Machines   26

12 Questions to Ask Before Pressing Start!   28
- 10 More Critical Questions   29

Chapter 2: Lean Lines   30

- White Cotton Blouse   32
- Tobacco Sheath   36
- Fine Knit Cardigan Sweater   40
- Embellished Jeans   44
- Blue Jacket   48
- Tweed Suit   56

Chapter 3: Notable Necklines   60

- Red Pullover   62
- Brown Corduroy Jacket   66
- Sheer Organdy Blouse   70

Chapter 4: Classy Collars and Cuffs   74

- Floral Jeans   76
- Capri Pants   82
- Silk Blouse   86

Chapter 5: Princely Pockets   92

- Simple Monogram   94
- Romantic Monogram   98
- Heirloom Monogram   102
- Teal Jacket   106

Chapter 6: Exotic Edges   110

- Robin's Egg Blue Dress with Bias Ruffle   112
- Green Knit Pullover Shirt   116
- Khaki Peplum Jacket   122
- Sweatshirt   128

Resources   134

Acknowledgments   136

About the Author   137

CD-ROM Embroidery Designs   138

Index   140

Chapter 1 Tips, Tricks and Techniques

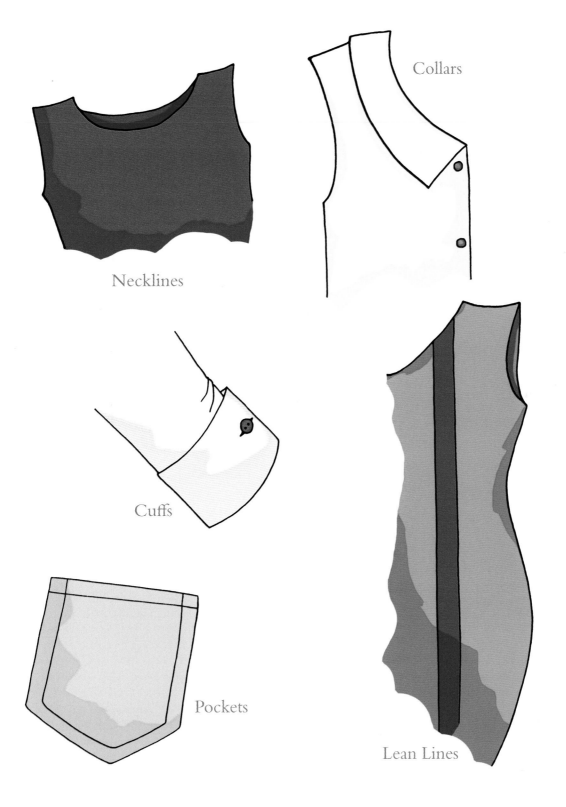

Necklines

Collars

Cuffs

Pockets

Lean Lines

Fashion Fundamentals for Machine Embroidery

In the following pages, you will learn to turn the mundane into the fabulous! Well, maybe not fabulous but definitely more interesting. Machine embroidery is a wonderful tool for making a personal statement, updating a plain wardrobe or showcasing your talent.

Using Blanks

Like any great artist, your embroidery must start with a blank canvas. In the embroidery industry, this is called a blank. Common blanks readily available to the commercial industry are T-shirts, golf shirts, caps, aprons and uniforms. Let's take a closer look at blanks that are more fashionable than the industry standard offerings. They include jeans, pants, jackets, blouses, fitted T-shirts, dresses and skirts.

What to Look for in a Blank

As a general rule for purchasing blanks, look for:
- high-quality fabrics
- open areas to place the embroidery
- few tailored details

Always purchase the highest-quality garment you can afford. A cheaply made garment will not look any better with embroidery.

Garments with open areas present fewer challenges to the embroiderer, and embroidery tends to improve the overall appearance of such garments.

Avoid garments that have welt pockets, flat-felled seams, curvy princess seams and impossible-to-detach linings and facings. The multiple layers of fabric that make up welt pockets and flat-felled seams can be difficult to hoop, as they do not allow the even distribution of tension in the hoop. The use of adhesive stabilizers enables you to hoop garments with welt pockets and flat-felt seams; however, professional results are achieved when stitching on a single layer of fabric. Avoid placing embroidery on the bulky areas and keep the embroidery a safe distance from the multiple layers so that the embroidery foot does not get caught in the bulk.

Curvy princess seams are quite flattering on many figures, but the curvier the curve, the more difficult it is to press the fabric flat so the embroidery can be stitched. It's possible, but challenging.

Turn the garment inside out and examine the lining and facing. Does the lining hang free at the hem? If so, it's the perfect candidate for embroidery since you can easily hoop the garment while keeping the lining out of the design area. If the lining is attached at the hem, see if removing a few stitches at the hem will enable you to separate it from the garment.

Check the facing. Can you pull it away from the body of the garment, enabling you to hoop one layer? Can you maneuver around the permanent stitching of buttonholes?

Skirts

Look for:
- A-line or straight skirts
- Free-hanging lining
- Focal points on pieced skirts, yoke waistbands and gores
- Straight border area or ruffled hems

Avoid:
- Circle skirts (so much fabric calls for hours of embroidery)
- Bias skirts (dense embroidery can hinder the gentle drape of a bias skirt)

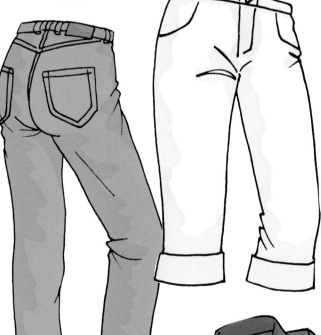

Pants

Look for:
- Flattering fit
- Flat front for midriff embroidery
- No pockets
- Side or back opening
- Faced waistbands
- Removable linings

Avoid:
- Flat-felled seams on the outside of the leg
- Novelty details, such as sewn-in belts and buckles
- Rivets

Jackets

Look for:
- Open areas
- Unlined or detachable linings
- Interesting lines
- Sleeve cuffs
- Generous collars

Avoid:
- Welt pockets
- Two-piece sleeves
- Excessive topstitching
- Curvy princess seams

Cardigans

Look for:

- Simple, clean lines
- Solid colors
- Plain, knitted borders

Avoid:

- Existing embellishment
- Skin-tight fit
- Chunky knitted texture

Sweatshirts, Blouses and Pullovers

Look for:

- High-quality fabric
- Pleasing color
- Flattering fit

Avoid:

- Facings
- Snaps and eyelets

Dresses

Look for:

- High-quality fabric with natural fibers
- Timeless style
- Detachable linings
- Open areas for embellishment

Avoid:

- Full skirts
- Excessive details like belts, pockets, topstitching, etc.
- Heavily beaded areas

Dealing with Notions

Some notions and trimmings on ready-to-wear garments present problems to embroiderers and others we can simply ignore.

Snaps and Rivets

Most snaps and rivets cannot be removed without damaging the garment. When stitched on, these items definitely will break the needle if they come in contact with it. Avoid placing embroidery near these notions.

Buttons

Buttons can be temporarily or permanently removed. Snip them off if your embroidery will land dangerously close to the button, and sew it back on later. If the button and buttonholes interfere with your embroidery layout, permanently eliminate them. Stitch the buttonholes closed or cover them with an embroidery design or length of ribbon.

Beads

Beads are beautiful when paired with the silky sheen of embroidery, but it's easier to add the beads after embroidering. Trying to plan embroidery designs around existing beads is time-consuming and frustrating. Avoid purchasing beaded garments as blanks.

buttons

embroidery designs

pearl centers

Designing the Embroidery Layout

Once the garment, or canvas, is selected, it's time to design the layout of the embroidery. Take into consideration what you are comfortable wearing. If most of your garments are plain, then you would probably be more comfortable in clothing with subtle touches of embroidery. This can be achieved through both quantity and color. If, on the other hand, your closet is full of bold, embellished fashions, then you would be right at home with a heavy splattering of stitches on your embroidered garment. Some things to take into consideration are your favorite colors, favorite style, body type and lifestyle.

Armed with that personal information, it's time to doodle. Where is your first inclination to place the embroidery? Most likely, that's the most interesting feature of the blank. Start designing your embroidery layout there. On a sheath, it might be the long, lean line. On a jacket, it could be generously proportioned sleeve cuffs. Or maybe nothing calls to you when looking at a plain, pullover shirt. Here your challenge is to create a focal point.

1. Select a sketch from the provided drawings on the previous two pages that best resembles the garment you are designing.

TIP

There is no need to be an artist. A simple line can represent a zipper, a square is a pocket and a circle becomes a button.

2. Lay a sheet of tracing paper over the drawing and trace it.

3. Fit as many repeats on the page as possible (six is a good number to start with).

4. Compare your garment to the sketch.

5. Add any pertinent details, such as pockets, seams, buttons, zippers, etc., to the drawing.

Materials

- Tracing paper
- Pencil
- Time to doodle

Letting the Garment Guide You

The Brown Jacket on pages 66 through 69 is a great example of symmetrical embroidery with identical right and left front sides.

The Fine Knit Cardigan Sweater on pages 40 through 43 shows how attractive an asymmetrical embroidery design can look on a symmetrical garment.

Add narrow, vertical design areas to long, linear silhouettes such as sheaths, cigarette pants and pencil skirts.

Jackets

Symmetrical Embroidery: Treat both right and left identically. Design one side of the jacket and then mirror-image everything on the opposite side.

Symmetrical Garment-Asymmetrical Embroidery: Instead of duplicating the embroidery from the right front to the left front, add more interest by adding different layouts. The key to success in designing an asymmetrical embroidery layout is balancing the quantity and color of the embroidery. Divide the garment in horizontal thirds and then divide each third in half down the center front of the garment. This will give you six areas to use as a grid for placing the embroidery designs.

Here are two of my favorite layouts for asymmetrical embroidery (Figures 1-1 and 1-2).

Figure 1-1: *The sketch above illustrates the rule of three. This garment keeps the viewer's eye moving around the jacket and eventually the eyes will rest on the wearer's face. The placement of the embroidery also avoids creating a horizontal focus. Horizontal embroidery widens the girth of the wearer and is flattering on a limited number of figures. Although there are some tricks to slenderizing the figure by placing horizontal embroidery in a high or low position, it can be difficult to achieve.*

Figure 1-2: *Here, the midsections of the grid are divided into even smaller areas. First, it's split in half and then each half is split into two more sections. Now there are a total of eight small sections in the middle of the torso.*

Putting the Sketch into Reality

1. Print templates of the designs to embroider and audition them on the fabric, using the sketch as a guide.

2. Tape them to the garment.

3. Put the garment on and stand in front of a mirror. Examine the placement of the designs.

4. Move templates so they can be seen, if necessary.

Helpful hints for choosing design placement:
- If the embroidery crosses a seam, such as a shoulder or armhole, the addition of heavy stitches can eliminate any stretch that exists in the seam.
- Wherever you place the embroidery, you create a focal point. Make sure it's one you want to draw attention to.
- Not every garment benefits from the addition of embroidery. Truly classic separates rarely look better with embroidery.

Now that you know what to look for in a blank, it's time to gather your tools and learn some new tips and tricks before you start stitching.

The Blue Jacket on pages 48 through 55 shows another option for asymmetrical designs on a symmetrical garment. Here, I placed the embroidery in flipped mirror-image. The layout on the upper left bodice is almost the same as the layout on the lower right bodice, but this time, the layouts overlap in the middle section. Notice how the embroidery on the upper left bodice extends to the waist. This helps elongate the figure. This can also be achieved by extending the embroidery on the lower right up past the waist. When doing this, the focus then is brought to one breast, which is not very desirable, as it makes most women feel self-conscious.

Embroidery Designs

There are thousands of embroidery designs available. You can find them in your embroidery machine, at your local dealership and on the Internet. They are available on CD (like the designs included in this book), floppy disk, flash stick, memory card, wireless connectivity and direct connection with a computer. They come in many popular formats including ART, DST, EXP, JEF, PES, SHV and XXX, among others. Read your embroidery machine manual to determine the format and media your machine requires.

With so many designs to choose from, where do you start? I like to start at the end! The first thing I think of when selecting embroidery designs is where to use them. Knowing where I'm going to use a design helps narrow down the selection by the process of elimination. When I'm embroidering on wearables—fashionable clothing—there are a few factors to consider.

The artistic style of the design: Cartoon-like designs are wonderful on children's garments, but not on something many adults would wear. Gravitate toward more sophisticated or whimsical designs.

The dimension of the design: Designs that overlap, link together and are compatible with the style of the garment are my first choice. I seldom use medallion-type designs, the kind found in most commercial logos, on clothing. The closed figure of a medallion-type of design does not lend itself to interesting embroidery combinations.

The density of a design: I prefer light density designs in fashion embroidery because they lie on the fabric more fluidly. Bulletproof embroidery is fine for golf caps but

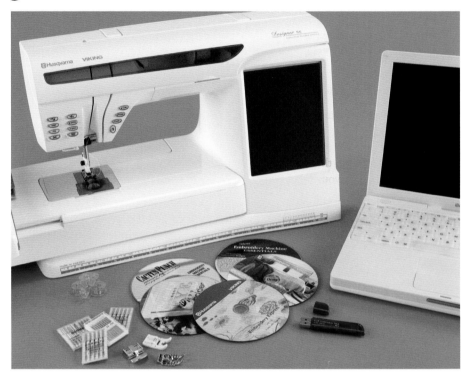

is not welcomed on a feminine ensemble.

The detail of a design: Fashion embroidery takes great liberty with artistic license. Here, a flower does not need every realistic petal, leaf and stem to tell the viewer it's a flower. Less is more in fashion embroidery.

The embroidery designs in this book were created for fashion embroidery—specifically for certain areas of a garment. While sketching the garments and designs, I kept my focus on you. I tried to create embroidery you would be proud to wear, designs that add an artistic flair to clothing while eliminating unnecessarily high stitch counts. This collection of embroidery designs will get you started on your journey of creating fashionable machine-embroidered garments.

Preparing the Designs

You will need an embroidery editing software program (also known as customizing software) with the following features:
- Copy and Paste
- Sizing with recalculating stitches
- 360-degree rotation
- Mirror-image
- Color Sort
- View by Color
- Lasso Tool
- Sew Simulator
- Print

Some familiar brands are Buzz Tools, BuzzEdit, Stitch Editor (Husqvarna Viking), Bernina Editor, PE-Design (Brother), Generations, Origins, Explorations (OESD), Designer's Gallery Studio (Baby Lock), Pfaff Creative Stitch Editor, Digitizer 10000 (Janome), Professional Sew Ware (Singer), Amazing Designs Smart Sizer Gold, Smart Sizer Platinum and Edit 'N Stitch.

Choosing a Design

1. Insert the *Contemporary Machine-Embroidered Fashions* CD into your CD drive.

2. Open your embroidery software.

3. Go to File, Open (Figure 1-3).

4. Select the CD drive.

5. Select the folder with the format that is compatible with your machine.

Figure 1-4
- *The size of the design is 94 mm x 97 mm. This is helpful when determining if the design will fit in the allotted space.*
- *The position of the design in the sewing field or hoop is also listed. The default setting is in the center, 0 mm x 0 mm on the XY axis. If you move the design, the position of the design will also change.*
- *Also, the stitch count is visible (11,525), along with the number of color changes (seven).*

6. Select MEF14. Notice that the design name will be followed by a dot and the abbreviation of your format. Your embroidery software recognizes the dot and the abbreviation as an embroidery file. Let's look at some of the information on the screen (Figure 1-4).

7. Move the cursor onto the design and left-click to select the design. Notice the design has a "box" around it with a "handle" on each corner (Figure 1-5).

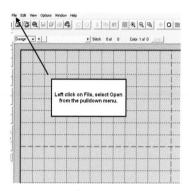

Left click on File, select Open from the pulldown menu.

Figure 1-3

Figure 1-5

Editing a Design

Once you have selected a design, there are several ways to create something different than the basic design.

Figure 1-6

Copy and Paste: Duplicates and merges separate embroidery designs into one file. Once you have clicked on the design to select it, go to File, Copy (or CTRL C), followed by File, Paste (or CTRL V) (Figure 1-6).

Drag the handle to make the design larger or smaller. Hold the shift key to maintain the proportions.

Figure 1-7

Sizing: Adjusts the size of an embroidery design while adding and subtracting stitches automatically. Hold the shift key, click on the embroidery design and drag one corner to make the design larger or smaller (Figures 1-7 and 1-8).

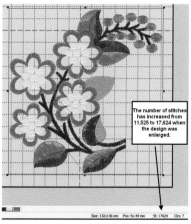

The number of stitches has increased from 11,525 to 17,624 when the design was enlarged.

Figure 1-8

Figure 1-9

Figure 1-10

Figure 1-11

Figure 1-12: *The image ready to be color-sorted.*

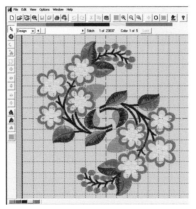

Figure 1-13: *After sorting, note how the color bar at the top has shifted from Figure 1-12.*

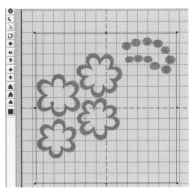

Figure 1-14

Holding the shift key will maintain the design proportions. Keep in mind that detail in an embroidery design is determined by its original size. A butterfly originally digitized at 2½" will look very simplistic when enlarged to 4½". The opposite is true, too; a highly detailed butterfly digitized at 4½" will be too "busy" at 2½".

Rotation: Spins the design. To use, click on the rotation tool (Figure 1-9), click on the embroidery design to select it and move one corner of the design in the desired direction (Figure 1-10).

Mirror-Image: Makes a horizontal or vertical mirror-image of the design. To use, click on the embroidery design to select it and click on the mirror im-age tool, which has a vertical or horizontal option (Figure 1-11).

Color Sort: Merges all like colors into one color segment (Figures 1-12 and 1-13). It is especially helpful when repeating the same design in one hoop. To use, Copy and Paste the designs onto the screen in the desired positions. Click on Color Sort. This option should be used with caution as the sequencing of the color segments can be affected. Use the Sew Simulator to check for accuracy if the software program has that feature. As a rule of thumb, designs that contain the same colors and overlap may cause trouble when the Color Sort feature is used. If the designs do not overlap, Color Sort will eliminate unnecessary thread changes.

View by Color: Lets you travel through the design color segment by color segment. Also lets you select, re-move or duplicate a segment. To use, click on the design to select it and click on the View By Color tool. Click on the tool to travel through the design (Figure 1-14).

Organizing and Storing Your Designs

For all embroidery collections, purchase a three-ring binder, CD and floppy disk storage sleeves, and a three-hole punch from any office supply store. Upon opening a disk collection, punch holes in the artwork (packaging and thread list if applicable). Insert the artwork in the binder and the CD or floppy into the storage sleeve. As time passes, you'll love going to the binder and easily locating the exact collection.

It's also helpful to organize your designs in your computer. Here is how I organized my hard drive for creating this book:

1. To access the C drive (the hard drive), go to Start, My Computer. Then double left-click on the icon for the C drive (Figure 1-15).

2. Right-click on the screen, select New, Folder and type in "Embroidery Designs" (Figure 1-16).

3. Organize files by collection or category in this folder (Figure 1-17). I've listed some collections by name, such as the Designs Interactive CD 1, 2 and 3. Other files are labeled Flowers, Trees, Animals, Geometrics and so on. Each of the folders has subcategories when opened.

Let's take a look in the *Machine-Embroidered Fashions* folder. Double left-click on the folder to open it. Each category, or chapter, in *Machine-Embroidered Fashions* is listed by name (Figure 1-18).

I've stored all of the original designs and manipulated designs required for that category. In doing this, some designs are in multiple locations. Let's look in the Notable Necklines folder. Every design featured in that category is in that folder (Figure 1-19).

When I start a new project, I create a new folder with the project name. Then I open my embroidery software and access the designs from their original source, which could be another file from the main Embroidery Design folder, CD or floppy disk. As I manipulate the designs, I save them in the new folder.

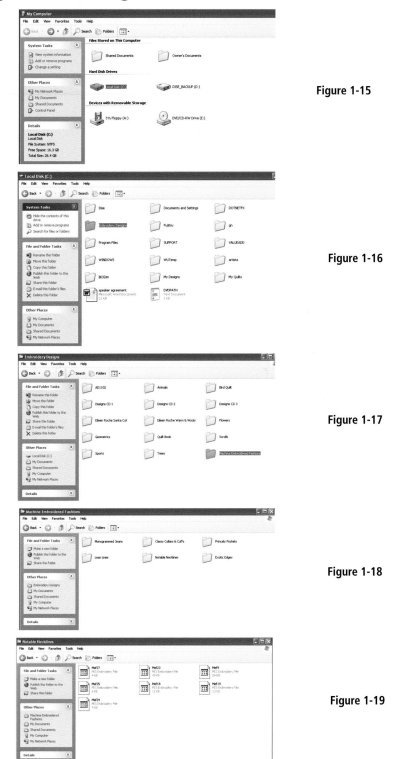

Figure 1-15

Figure 1-16

Figure 1-17

Figure 1-18

Figure 1-19

Templates: Your Road Map to Success

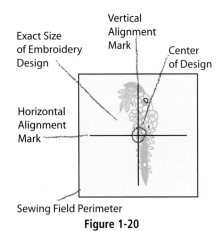

Exact Size of Embroidery Design

Vertical Alignment Mark

Center of Design

Horizontal Alignment Mark

Sewing Field Perimeter

Figure 1-20

What is a Template?

A template is a printed image of the embroidery design in actual size centered in the sewing field (Figure 1-20). The best feature about templates is there are no surprises—the location of the design is predictable and planned. Templates ensure positive and professional results in all of your embroidery projects.

Templates also provide perfect placement of embroidery designs. No more guesswork; the design will stitch exactly where you planned when you use templates.

How Do You Use Templates?

There are two areas of focus when working with embroidery designs. When designing or planning a project, the focus is on the outer edges of an embroidery design—where one design ends and the next one begins.

The second area of focus is the center of the embroidery design. The center of the design is where the needle is located in the sewing field once the design is selected on the machine.

Using Target Stickers with Templates

If you use a template in the planning stage and position the needle over the template's crosshair, you are guaranteed perfect placement. The design will stitch in the exact location that you planned. However, templates can be unwieldy during the hooping process and multiple templates taped on a hooped garment can get in the way of the needle.

I use target stickers to designate the center of the embroidery design. These small, pressure-sensitive dots have a

TIP

Today, many embroidery machines let you select needle placement when a design is chosen (Figure 1-21). You may choose to place the needle in the lower left corner, upper right corner or other location.

This feature is helpful when confirming the placement of a design. Use it when you're concerned about a design fitting in a confined area (such as a cuff) or connecting with an existing design.

I have my machines set with the needle in the center when a design is selected. I change it only when I want to check on the outer dimension of the design.

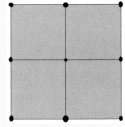

Figure 1-21

crosshair printed on them. Here's how to use them:

1. Slide the target sticker under the template, aligning the crosshairs and positioning the sticker's arrow in the same direction as the top of the embroidery design.

2. Remove the template; the center is marked by the reusable sticker.

3. Attach the hoop to the machine and move the needle to the center of the crosshair, using the alignment marks on the embroidery foot as a guide.

4. Remove the target sticker once you are satisfied with the placement and embroider the design.

Where Do You Get Templates?

In your embroidery software, open the desired design. Insert paper, tracing paper or a transparency into the printer. Go to File, Print.

Plastic templates normally have a hole for marking the center of the design and are virtually indestructible (unless you leave them on the dashboard of an automobile on a hot day).

Paper Templates

Pros
- Inexpensive
- Easy to write on
- Provides actual design size

Cons
- Opaque
- Having to cut around the image

Transparency Templates

Pros
- Provides actual design size
- Translucent

Cons
- Expensive
- Images can smear

Tracing Paper Templates

Pros
- Relatively inexpensive
- Provides actual design size
- Easy to write on
- Translucent

Cons
- Difficult to feed through printer

Manufactured Templates

Some manufacturers include embroidery templates with collections. I designed three collections for Amazing Designs that include templates printed on vellum. Vellum is similar to tracing paper, but it is a bit stronger, which means vellum templates enjoy a longer lifespan.

Other embroidery collections have plastic templates that are included with the collection or available separately.

Paper Templates

Transparency Templates

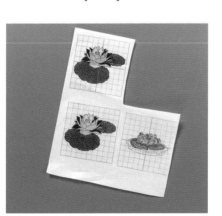

Tracing Paper Templates

Manufactured Templates

TIP

If the tracing paper is larger than 8½" x 11", trim the width to 8½". Tape one short edge of the tracing paper to a sheet of regular copy paper. Insert the two sheets into the printer, taped edge first, making sure the tracing paper will receive the ink.

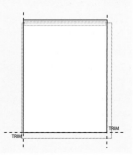

Stabilizer

It can be quite challenging to select a stabilizer when there are so many choices. Let's start by asking a few questions that will help you pare down the selection.

Q: Will the wrong side of the embroidery be visible?

A: If so, a tear-away or completely removable stabilizer would be the first choice.

Q: Is a permanent stabilizer required? And why would it need to be permanent?

A: All knits and heavily laundered items, such as uniforms and athletic wear, require a stabilizer that remains in the design to maintain the crispness of a design's details. A permanent stabilizer also helps retain the design's shape after repeated washings.

Q: Is the fabric sheer?

A: Embroidering on tulle, organdy, netting and other sheer fabrics requires completely removable stabilizer.

Q: Is the fabric translucent, such as light-colored knits and wovens?

A: Stabilizer bleed-through is a fashion no-no! Choose a tear-away or light cut-away, such as polymesh, to avoid that halo effect.

Q: Can the fabric withstand water or heat applications?

A: Velvet, silks and other delicate fabrics require special attention.

Q: Will the act of tearing the excess stabilizer distort the fabric or embroidery design?

A: Ripping the stabilizer off the embroidery design can damage delicate fabrics and embroidery outlines. Check the tear-away product itself. Does it tear easily and cleanly in both directions?

Q: Is the item wearable?

A: The stabilizer should provide a foundation for the embroidery without changing the drape of the fabric.

Q: Is this a multiple-item project (or large production run)?

A: Tear-aways tend to save time on repeat applications.

Q: What is the stitch count of the embroidery design?

A: Light and airy designs can be produced with high definition with a minimum of stabilizer, while large fill designs require a stronger foundation.

Q: Can the item fit in a hoop?

A: Hooping ensures the best stabilization for any fabric. Difficult or impossible-to-hoop items require an adhesive backing or, at the very least, the addition of a temporary spray adhesive.

Q: Does the fabric have a pile and will the application of an adhesive pull on the pile or loops?

A: Lofty fabrics call for a topper (usually water-soluble film) to tame the nap so the stitches do not sink into the fabric. Adhesive stabilizers used as backing on pile fabrics can pull the fibers upon release. Protect the fabric with a fusible, light tear-away between the item and the sticky stabilizer.

There are so many variables in the embroidery process that a test should be conducted for every fabric, design and stabilizer. Some of the variables include: stability of the fabric; color of the fabric; design stitch count; thread type; needle choice; machine speed; stitch length; hooping technique; needle tension; and bobbin tension.

Use the questionnaire just mentioned to guide you in your initial selection of a stabilizer and then test the fabric/design/stabilizer combo. If you're satisfied with your initial selection, go with it. If not, change one variable and test again.

Keep your samples; they'll show the result of each adjustment you make. Write the results on an index card and staple it to the sample. If you don't have extra fabric from the project, purchase ¼-yard of similar fabric or go to a secondhand clothing store and buy a duplicate article.

Types of Stabilizers

Cut-away: These are best for knits and loosely woven fabrics. A permanent stabilizer, cut-away is trimmed to within a ¼" from the design edge.

It comes in a variety of weights, from lightweight (but strong) polymesh to heavy. Select a weight that will support the design without changing the hand of the fabric.

Cut-away should not be visible from the right side of the embroidery. Polymesh cut-away is available in black, white and beige, while many other cut-aways are available in white and black.

Many cut-aways are fusible products and if not, they work very well with temporary spray adhesive.

Tear-away: Best for woven fabrics, a tear-away stabilizer should be easy to remove. Just pull on the excess stabilizer and the needle perforations from the embroidery will help release the excess. Tear-away should tear in both directions. When selecting a tear-away, give it a pull in both directions.

Tear-away remains in the design, providing a foundation for the embroidery throughout the life of the item. Tear-away should only be used on designs and fabrics that can withstand the violent act of tearing the excess. It's difficult to remove tear-away from small open areas within a design. Use it with medallion-type designs. Delicate fabrics and light, airy designs are not good candidates for tear-away.

Wash-away: Can be used as both a backing and topper. It is available in many forms today: plastic film, paper, liquid and woven. Regardless of its form, all wash-aways are completely removable when wetted. The number one factor in deciding whether to use a wash-away is asking if the fabric can get wet. And not only can it get wet, but do you have the time to wet and dry the fabric?

Wash-away film comes in a variety of weights; light is excellent as a topper and heavy is the best foundation for lace, edging and cutwork. Read the manufacturer's directions for removal. Different manufacturers do different things. Some call for hot (watch out for fabric shrinkage), cool or tepid water.

When used as a topper, lightweight wash-away can be gently torn away from the embroidery. Small patches can be removed with a dampened cotton swab or toothbrush.

Heat-away: Best for non-washable fabrics, sheer fabrics and fabrics too delicate for a tear-away, heat-away stabilizers come in two forms: film and woven. They are completely removable when applied in the correct manner. The film version of heat-away is removed with a dry iron and is often used as a topper. The woven version is great for lace-making or creating fabric with thread. It will crumble when heated with a dry iron. Follow the manufacturer's directions for best results.

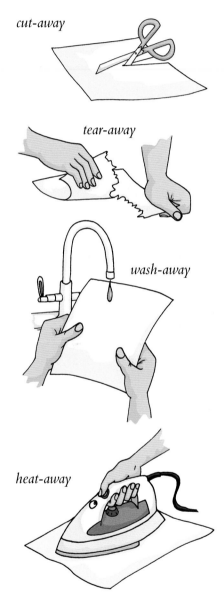

cut-away

tear-away

wash-away

heat-away

TIP

Although many embroiderers insist on using only one layer of stabilizer, I find two layers of a light tear-away are easier to remove than one layer of heavy tear-away. This is a matter of personal preference. See what works best for you.

Threads

Thread is the embroiderer's paint. Use it to color your life—and your embroidery! Rayon, polyester and cotton threads are readily available for the home embroiderer in a wide array of colors. Most embroidery designs are digitized for 40-wt., two-ply, rayon embroidery threads. Since thread comes in many fibers and weights, it's important to know what type you're work-

ing with. Keep in mind, the larger the weight number, the lighter the thread.

Rayon thread: Has a unique, tight twist that produces a radiant sheen. Available in hundreds of colors, rayon thread is strong, pliable and durable. Use it for all clothing except those that must be laundered with chlorine bleach.

Polyester thread: Resists breakage and abrasion and retains its brilliance

after repeated washings. Unlike rayon, polyester thread can be laundered with soap containing brighteners and chlorine bleach.

Cotton thread: Presents a soft, matte-like appearance in embroidery. Select cotton embroidery thread when you want to create an "Old World" feel that is natural and warm in appearance.

Basic Hooping Technique

Many *Designs in Machine Embroidery* readers tell me the most challenging part of the embroidery process is hooping. If the item is not hooped properly, disappointment is waiting in the wings. And many times, you feel you did everything right. The fabric was "square" in the hoop and tight as a drum, and yet, when the item was released, puckers appeared! Yikes! What went wrong?

I'll bet that you hooped the item, tightened the screw (maybe even with a screwdriver!), tugged on the fabric for a snug fit and stitched away. Well, it's not that simple. There's another step and an absolute "don't" to take into consideration. The extra step is setting the proper hoop tension and the "don't" is: Don't ever tug on the fabric once it's hooped.

Setting Proper Hoop Tension

1. Loosen the screw of the outer hoop.

2. Place the outer hoop on a flat, hard surface.

3. Place the stabilizer(s) and fabric on the outer hoop.

4. Place the inner hoop on the fabric, making sure the alignment marks on both the outer and inner hoops line up.

5. Press the end opposite the screw into the outer hoop with the palm of your hand.

6. Work both palms around the hoop until the entire inner hoop is in position (Figure 1-23).

7. Tighten the screw by hand (no need for a screwdriver) until it becomes difficult to turn. Do not pull on the fabric.

8. Remove the inner hoop. Now that the inner hoop is removed, the tension is evenly distributed around the entire hoop, not concentrated at the location of the screw.

Figure 1-23

Hooping

1. Lay the template of the embroidery design in the desired location on the fabric and tape the template in position.

2. Place the inner hoop on the fabric, aligning the hoop's horizontal and vertical centering marks with the crosshair on the template.

3. Pick up the fabric and hoop with both hands, holding the hoop in position.

4. Place one end of the inner hoop into the outer hoop, hold in place and insert the other end of the hoop.

5. Press firmly on both ends of the hoop with the palms of your hands (Figure 1-24).

6. Gently press the inner hoop slightly deeper than the outer hoop. This technique is called countersinking and allows the fabric to sit on the machine bed without floating above the surface.

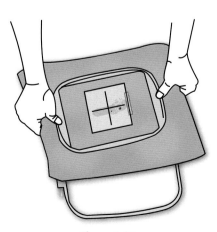

Figure 1-24

Helpful Tools

I have often been frustrated at the lack of tools available for machine embroiderers. Great advances have been made in machine features, software and media, but little attention has been paid to the actual process of getting the fabric in the hoop and the design where you want it to land! I've created a few products I think you'll find helpful.

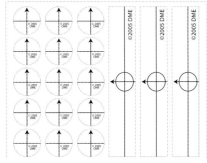

Target stickers

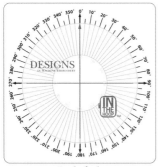

Angle finder

Target Stickers

Target stickers are small, pressure-sensitive adhesive stickers that eliminate the need to mark the fabric. Printed with a crosshair and an arrow, they can be used over and over again. Slide the target under a taped template, aligning the crosshair of the sticker with the template's crosshair. Once the sticker is secure, remove the template and hoop the fabric. Now you don't have to worry about shifting templates during the hooping process or erasing any marks left by "removable" markers.

Angle Finder

If you hoop the fabric incorrectly, the Angle Finder will tell you how much rotation is required to stitch the embroidery design as planned. With the combination of templates, target stickers and the Angle Finder, every design will stitch perfectly straight. Just follow these easy instructions for hooping wrong and stitching right! The Angle Finder works with any machine that features a one-degree or five-degree rotation.

Use the Angle Finder on Single Designs

1. Position a template and target sticker on the fabric in the desired location.

2. Hoop the fabric; don't worry about hooping perfectly square.

3. Center the Angle Finder on the target sticker with the zero-degree facing towards the upper edge of the hoop (Figure 1-25).

4. Keep the Angle Finder's black crosshair square to the hoop's outer edges.

5. Rotate the dial on the Angle Finder so the red crosshair is aligned with the target sticker (Figure 1-26).

6. Note the rotation degree that the red arrow designates. Make sure both arrows (target sticker and red crosshair) are facing in the same direction (Figure 1-27).

7. Rotate the design on the screen using the rotation keys until you reach the number as illustrated on the Angle Finder.

8. Embroider the design.

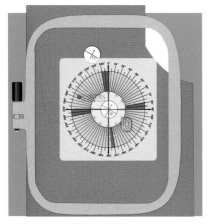

Figure 1-25

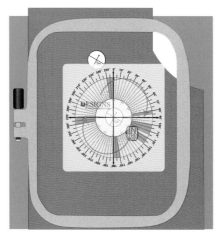

Figure 1-26

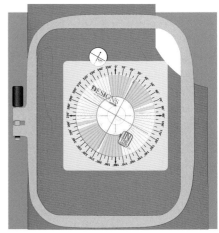

Figure 1-27

Centering Rulers

Use a centering ruler to measure the size of stitched designs, distances between existing designs, and to mark vertical and horizontal positioning lines. The rulers work on both flat surfaces and in the hoop. Their flexibility allows you to accurately measure inside the restricted area of a hoop. Their translucency enables you to see existing markings, target stickers, embroidery designs or sewn seams clearly.

Measure Stitched Designs in the Hoop

Gently lay the ruler over the hoop's edge while holding the ruler flat inside of the hoop (Figure 1-28).

Repeat a Pattern

1. Measure the size of the stitched design and divide by two.

2. Measure the distance between the two designs.

3. Add half the design size measurement plus the distance between the designs to find the center point for the third design.

4. Place that measurement on the outer edge of the second design and place a target sticker on the zero mark (Figure 1-29).

5. Center the needle over the target sticker crosshair, remove the sticker and embroider the design.

Continuous Hoop Designs

Even if you don't have a continuous hoop, you can still create continuous hoop designs with a Centering Ruler.
1. Stitch the first design.

2. Measure the design by placing one outer edge of the design on the zero.

3. Note the size (3½") and divide that number by two (1¾").

4. Place a target sticker on the 1¾" mark on the opposite side of the zero (Figure 1-31).

5. Move the fabric in the hoop so the target sticker is located under the needle.

6. Embroider the design and repeat the process.

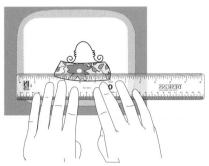

Figure 1-28

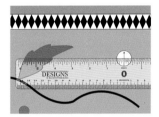

Figure 1-29

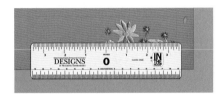

Figure 1-30

Figure 1-31

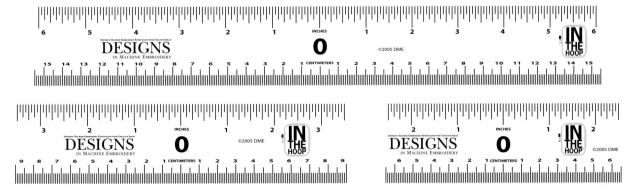

Three types of centering rulers specifically designed for use in machine embroidery.

Machines

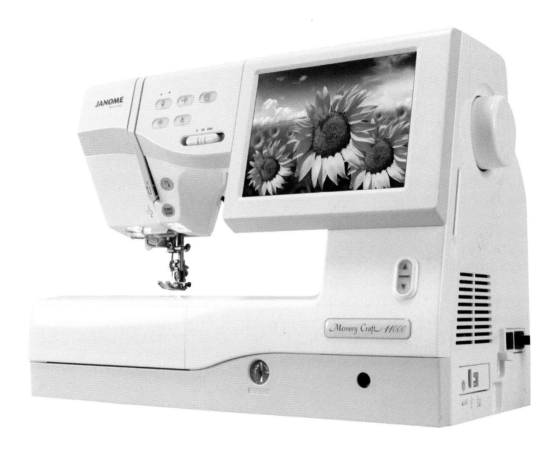

There are many embroidery machines available today with prices ranging from $300 to more than $8,000.

Why such a disparity in price?

Answer: The features. An embroidery machine can be a stand-alone unit or a combination of sewing and embroidery. It can have a computer built inside or be powered by a desktop or laptop computer. A home embroidery machine will have one needle and can accommodate a number of hoop sizes.

So where does one start when purchasing an embroidery machine? The best option is to find one right in your hometown. Embroidery machines can be highly technical—a helpful, knowledgeable dealer who is geographically close to you is helpful. Don't necessarily shop by brand; shop by dealer. Visit several local dealers and select the one who offers education, has on-site repairs and is someone you enjoy visiting.

Then test drive! Decide what features are important to you, then sit down at several models in your price range. Take the machine through some common tasks, such as selecting an embroidery design and making a few on-screen editing tasks. If you feel comfortable with the screen, the layout, the keys, etc., this could be the machine for you.

There are many features that entice embroiderers. Here are a few of my favorites.

Media: I love an embroidery machine that accepts a USB memory stick because it goes right from my computer to the machine. And I'm looking forward to a universal wireless transfer in the future.

Hoop size: A 5" x 7" sewing field is the smallest field I would consider when purchasing an embroidery machine. The larger sewing fields (7" x 10" and larger) are helpful but not mandatory, so skimp here if your budget is tight.

On-screen editing: A highly visible LCD screen makes selecting and editing designs a breeze. I like seeing the design on-screen in full color.

Perimeter tracing: This feature travels around the outermost edges of a design without taking a stitch. It's helpful when checking accuracy in placement.

Hoop movement: Since I do most of my design editing at my computer, the most important feature for me at the machine is the ability to position the needle over any spot in the hoop. I say, "position the needle" because the needle does not move, the hoop moves. And I want to see the needle positioned directly over a target sticker or template before I take a stitch.

One-degree rotation: I couldn't live without the ability to rotate in tiny increments.

Mirror-image: This cuts down on computer design and transfer time.

There are a few luxurious features that one may get accustomed to quite quickly. They are automatic threading systems, automatic thread trimmers, low bobbin indicators and the ability to read multi-formats.

Of course, the number one feature is the stitch quality. Your embroidery machine should present you with beautiful embroidery, so look for it when shopping for a new machine.

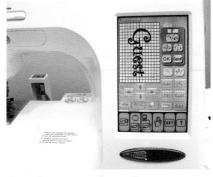

A one-degree rotation feature allows you to rotate each design ever-so-slightly.

Stitch quality should be your top priority when selecting an embroidery machine.

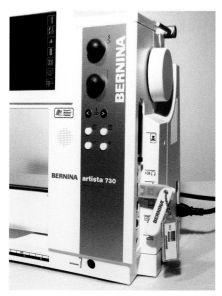

An embroidery machine that accepts a USB memory stick (shown here) allows for the convenience of quick transfer of designs from computer to machine.

A perimeter tracing feature helps to check the accuracy in placement.

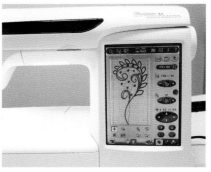

It is helpful to be able to see the design on-screen in full color.

12 Questions to Ask Before Pressing Start!

Whether you're a veteran embroiderer or a neophyte, it's important to remember simple steps lead to successful embroidery. You can avoid frustrating mistakes by asking yourself these 12 questions before you touch the start button on your embroidery machine.

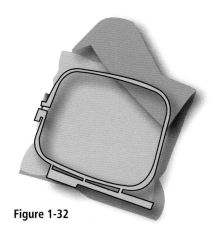

Figure 1-32

Figure 1-33

Q: Is the target sticker in the proper position?

A: If you're not sure, place the template back on the target sticker and double-check the position.

Q: Is a single layer of fabric hooped with the stabilizer?

A: As the inner hoop is forced into the outer hoop, extra layers of fabric can get caught. Always flip the hoop over and check the underside (Figure 1-32).

Q: Are there puckers in the hoop?

A: Run your finger across the surface of the fabric (Figure 1-33). If the fabric snowplows, it's too loose. Don't pull on the fabric; instead re-hoop it.

Q: Did you set the hoop tension?

A: Hoop your fabric and stabilizer. Hand-tighten the screw. At this point, all of the tension in the hoop is concentrated at the location of the screw (Figure 1-34). Release the inner hoop and hoop again, countersinking the inner hoop. Since there's no need to tighten the outer hoop, all of the tension is now evenly distributed around the hoop (Figure 1-35).

Q: Is the fabric taut like a tambourine?

A: Tap the palm of your hand on the wrong side of hooped fabric. It should feel tight, like a drum.

Q: Does it need a topper?

A: Many fabrics require a topper. A topper helps the stitches stay on top of the fabric and stops them from sinking into the fabric. Typical fabrics that call for a topper are terry cloth, fleece, fur and knits.

Q: Have you selected the desired design from the menu?

A: Check your chosen design carefully, as many designs look similar on the machine screen.

Q: Does the design on the screen match the template or does it need to be mirror-imaged or rotated?

A: Use the Angle Finder to determine the required rotation, if needed.

Q: Is the needle in the center of the target sticker?

A: Leave the target sticker in position and move the needle to the center of the crosshair (Figure 1-36).

Figure 1-34

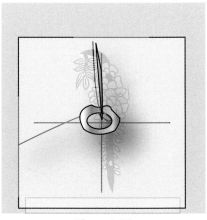

Figure 1-35

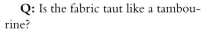

Figure 1-36

Q: Is the correct thread in the needle?

A: Check the color sequence and insert the correct thread. Nothing is worse than stitching black snow!

Q: Is anything obstructing the movement of the hoop?

A: Clear a space on your sewing table for the hoop to move freely. Lamps, stacks of fabric and notions can bump the frame and cause damage to your embroidery and machine.

Q: Did you remember to remove the target sticker before pressing the start button?

A: I have lots of target stickers with tiny needle holes stitched in them! Although it doesn't really hurt the adhesive markers, the needle most certainly doesn't like it!

Machine Tension

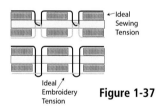

Figure 1-37

Note the proper look of machine embroidery from the wrong side when the tension is set correctly.

10 More Critical Questions

The true key to success in machine embroidery is testing embroidery designs with the selected fabric, stabilizer and thread. But what should you look for when testing? Use these 10 questions in your quest for perfect embroidery.

Q: Has the embroidery changed the hand of the fabric?

A: Consider the weight of the fabric when selecting embroidery designs. Dense designs with a high stitch count do not belong on delicate or stretchy fabrics.

Q: Is the bobbin thread visible on the right side of the embroidery?

A: Balanced thread tension for machine embroidery is different than balanced thread tension for sewing (Figure 1-37). Only one-third of the thread visible on the wrong side of the embroidery should be bobbin thread. The bobbin thread should never be visible on the right side of the embroidery.

Q: Is the fabric puckered?

A: Two solutions to the common problem of puckered fabric are improper hooping technique or insufficient stabilizer.

Q: Does the outline line up with the fill stitches?

A: If not, a new needle may be required or a stronger stabilizer is needed.

Q: Are there oversized holes from needle penetrations?

A: Select a needle appropriate for the fabric and you'll be happy with the results.

Q: Does the fabric bleed through the embroidery?

A: Increase the density of the design in embroidery software or add an opaque topper.

Q: Is the embroidery visible from a distance of six feet?

A: Use colors that "pop" or contrast with the base fabric. Black outlines help achieve this when using similar value thread and fabric. Monochromatic styles are elegant, but the embroidery should still be visible. Select thread that is two or three shades away from the base fabric.

Q: Is the stabilizer visible from the right side?

A: Many cut-away stabilizers show through light-colored fabrics. Select a polymesh cut-away when embroidering on these types of fabrics.

Q: Does the placement of the embroidery complement the figure of the model?

A: Consider the size and age of the model when placing embroidery. What's appropriate for a 12-year-old boy (shirttail embroidery) may not be in good taste for a 55-year-old woman.

Q: Does the placement of the embroidery enhance the overall design of the garment or detract from it?

A: Try the garment on and stand in front of a mirror. If you like what you see, you have done a great job of improving the garment. If not, audition more templates or consider adding decorative stitches to complete the design.

Sometimes, multiple tests are required to achieve professional embroidery. Make a test, analyze it, change only one element and stitch another test. If you change more than one element and still are not satisfied, you won't know what to change next. Keep your sample stitch-outs to use for future reference.

Once you tackle the small details, it's time to create the masterpiece!

Chapter 2 **Lean Lines**

Steps to Success . . .

- Fool the eye with color—use a single color from head to toe; or use dark on the bottom, light on the top.
- Keep the tailoring to a minimum; think less is more.
- Use the combo of dark shoes and slacks/skirts to create a longer line.
- Create slim, vertical spaces with decorative stitching, ribbon, trim and embroidery.
- Consider an asymmetrical design to narrow the silhouette.

Start with the Basics . . .

Fine Knit
Cardigan Sweater

Blue Jacket

White Cotton Blouse

Tweed Suit

Tobacco Sheath

Jeans

White Cotton Blouse

Satin-stitched vines enhance the vertical line

Materials

- White blouse
- 4 yd. ¼"-wide ribbon
- Water-soluble stabilizer, regular weight
- Temporary spray adhesive
- Target stickers
- Basic machine embroidery and sewing notions
- MEF3, MEF4 and MEF5 embroidery designs and templates

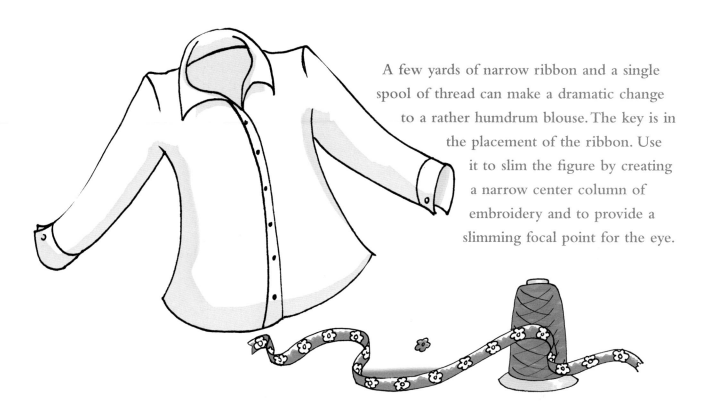

A few yards of narrow ribbon and a single spool of thread can make a dramatic change to a rather humdrum blouse. The key is in the placement of the ribbon. Use it to slim the figure by creating a narrow center column of embroidery and to provide a slimming focal point for the eye.

Plan the Design

1. Try on the blouse and stand in front of a mirror.

2. Take a length of ribbon and place it on the shoulder of the blouse, extending down the blouse front.

3. Move the ribbon to the right or left, stopping where you feel the ribbon is most flattering. On the sample, size medium, I found the ribbon looks best 5" from the center front.

4. Remove the blouse and lay it on a flat surface.

5. Measure the desired distance from the center front and lay the ribbon in a vertical line. If the blouse has a curved side seam, shape the ribbon parallel to the side seam, curving in at the waist and gently out at the hip.

6. Pin the ribbon in place and carefully lift it in sections to draw a faint line underneath the ribbon to mark the spot.

7. Audition the leaf templates inside the marked area.

8. Fill the design area keeping the leaves in a vertical pattern.

9. Envision a continuous vine (that you'll add after the embroidery) connecting all of the templates. Turning the leaves at odd angles can make it difficult to connect the leaves later with satin stitching.

10. Pin or tape the templates in place. Try the garment back on to make sure the embroidery designs do not lay right on the bust point.

11. Remove the blouse and lay it on a flat surface.

12. Slide target stickers under the templates.

13. Mark the design number and any instructions (such as mirror image) on each sticker.

Step 8: *Audition the leaf templates, filling the design area with leaves in a vertical pattern.*

Embroider the Shirt

Step 8: *Embroider the designs on the left front bodice.*

Step 10: *Embroider a similar set of leaves on the right front.*

1. Hoop two layers of water-soluble stabilizer and spray it with temporary adhesive.

2. Position the blouse on the sticky stabilizer, centering two or three templates. Smooth the fabric against the stabilizer, removing any wrinkles.

3. Pin the fabric to the stabilizer close to the edges of the hoop for added security.

4. Use the Angle Finder to determine the number of degrees to rotate the first design, if necessary. Refer to page 24 for more on the Angle Finder, if needed. Rotate the design on the screen as needed.

5. Position the needle over the first target sticker.

6. Remove the sticker and embroider the design. The leaf designs are machine appliqué designs, but in this project, don't add an appliqué fabric. Instead, omit color number one and stitch the remaining color segments.

7. Advance the needle to the second crosshair and embroider the design.

8. Repeat the process for all of the embroidery designs on the left front bodice.

9. Trim all thread tails.

10. Move to the right front and mimic the placement of the leaves on the left. It doesn't have to be an exact match. In fact, it's more interesting if the leaves are slightly different on each section.

11. Use Chalko-liner to draw a curving vine, connecting all the leaves.

12. Set up the machine for ordinary sewing and select the zigzag stitch. Program the stitch length to 0.4 mm and the stitch width to 2.7 mm.

13. Satin stitch on the drawn curvy line, locking the stitches when you reach a leaf.

14. Remove the water-soluble stabilizer by tearing away the large sections. Follow the manufacturer's directions for removing the remainder.

Attach the Ribbon

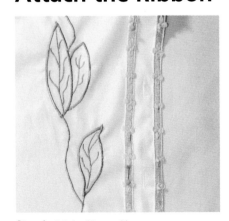

Step 1: *Stitch ribbon to blouse.*

Step 5: *Detail of one segment of the finished design.*

1. Pin the ribbon on the marked basting lines and sew the ribbon to the blouse.

2. Thread the needle with thread that matches the ribbon or monofilament.

3. Place a sheet of lightweight tear-away stabilizer under the stitching line.

4. Edgestitch on both sides of the ribbon or use a twin-needle.

5. Repeat steps 1 through 4 for the left and right fronts and the cuffs for the finished look shown.

Get the eye moving ... add embroidery in a vertical line

Monochromatic designs

Wear with:

- ෴ pinstriped pants for an updated look
- ෴ a chunky pearl necklace
- ෴ plain ballet slippers

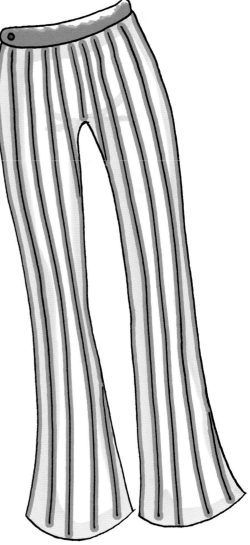

Tobacco Sheath

Accent the long, lean line with embroidery

Materials

- Unlined linen sheath
- Polymesh stabilizer (the length of the dress plus 8")
- ½"-wide ribbon, decorative cord or beaded trim, twice the length of the sheath
- Double-sided repositionable adhesive tape (Res-Q Tape)
- Angle Finder
- Target stickers
- Basic machine embroidery and sewing notions
- MEF20 embroidery design and seven to eight templates

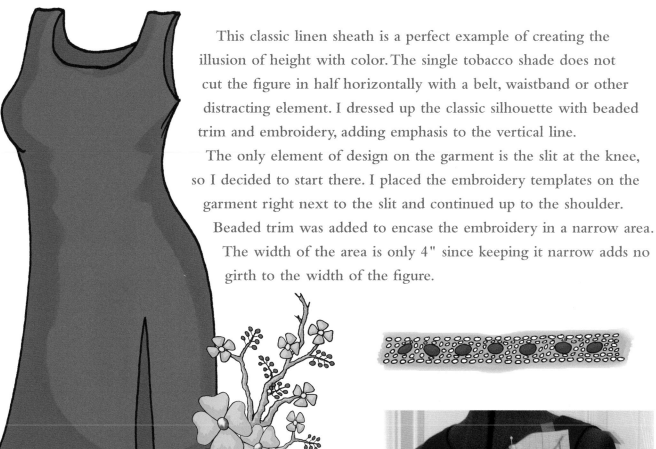

This classic linen sheath is a perfect example of creating the illusion of height with color. The single tobacco shade does not cut the figure in half horizontally with a belt, waistband or other distracting element. I dressed up the classic silhouette with beaded trim and embroidery, adding emphasis to the vertical line.

The only element of design on the garment is the slit at the knee, so I decided to start there. I placed the embroidery templates on the garment right next to the slit and continued up to the shoulder.

Beaded trim was added to encase the embroidery in a narrow area. The width of the area is only 4" since keeping it narrow adds no girth to the width of the figure.

Plan the Design

1. Try on the sheath and stand in front of a mirror to determine the most flattering position for a design area.

2. Pin two lengths of the trim at the shoulder to create a narrow, vertical space.

3. Audition the templates. To create the illusion of a continuous line of embroidery, butt the templates right next to each other. Mirror-imaging some of the designs (just flip the template over) will help the flow of the embroidery.

4. Carefully remove the dress.

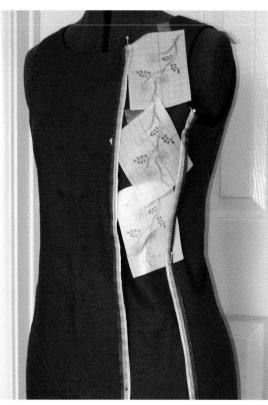

Step 3: *Use templates to plan the design.*

Embroider the Sheath

Note: The 60" length of polymesh stabilizer will stabilize the entire length of the design area.

1. Hoop one end of the stabilizer, allowing the remainder to flow down the length of the dress.

2. Open the zipper and turn the dress inside out.

3. Lift the facing at the neck away from the dress and pin the dress to the stabilizer, centering the first template by the neckline.

4. Attach the hoop to the machine, carefully placing the dress around the bed of the machine. Make sure only a single layer of the dress is in the sewing field.

5. Embroider the first design.

6. Move the needle to the center of the second target sticker.

7. Use the Angle Finder to determine the required rotation of the design. Refer to page 24 for more on the Angle Finder, if needed.

8. Rotate the design on the screen.

9. Embroider the second design.

10. Remove the hoop from the machine and the garment from the hoop.

11. Continue the embroidery process as in steps 6 through 10, but hoop both the dress and the stabilizer whenever possible.

12. Enlarge the last two designs to fill the space if a gap is left at the hem area. Print new templates and tape them to the dress. Make sure the size difference is almost indiscernible to the eye. Hang the dress on a door and step back 10 feet. If you can't see the difference, no one else will.

Step 6: *Move the needle in preparation for the design repeat.*

Using Beaded Tape

Beads add wonderful texture and dimension to embroidery, but often we're short on time and the task of beading by hand is not an option. Look for beaded tape in the trimming department of your local fabric store. Use it as accent, but be careful of the ends of the tape. They must be secured so that the whole tape will not unravel. Follow these easy steps.

Step 1: *Remove all beads from a ½" section at the tape end.*

Step 2: *Sew the empty section to a ribbon, ½" from the ribbon end.*

Step 3: *Fold the ribbon over the empty section of the beaded tape and sew.*

Step 4: *Cut the ribbon, leaving a ½" tail.*

Step 5: *Fold under the raw edge of the ribbon, fold the remainder of the ribbon back on itself and stitch to secure all edges.*

Attach the Trim

1. Pin the trim to the dress, centering the embroidery.

2. Sew the trim in place or in the case of beaded trim, use a removable tape. Res-Q Tape is a double-sided repositionable adhesive tape for fabric.

3. Apply the tape to the dress then finger-press the beaded trim to the sticky surface, turning the finished edge of the tape to the wrong side of the garment for the finished look shown.

4. Remove the trim and tape when it's time to launder the garment.

5. Apply a new strip to the trim after the garment is cleaned.

Step 3: *Detail of finished design with beaded trim.*

Elegant, Timeless Design

Wear with:

- turquoise clutch
- straw hat
- flat, beaded sandals

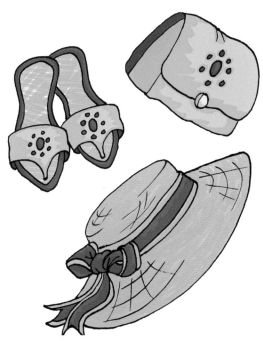

Fine Knit Cardigan Sweater

Delicate and sweet appliqué … light, fast and elegant

Materials

- Beige sweater cardigan
- 10 hot pink and apple green 4" square scraps tulle
- Polymesh stabilizer
- Tricot knit interfacing
- Robison Anton thread
- Temporary spray adhesive
- Target stickers
- Basic machine embroidery and sewing notions
- MEF1, MEF2, MEF10 and MEF26 embroidery designs and templates

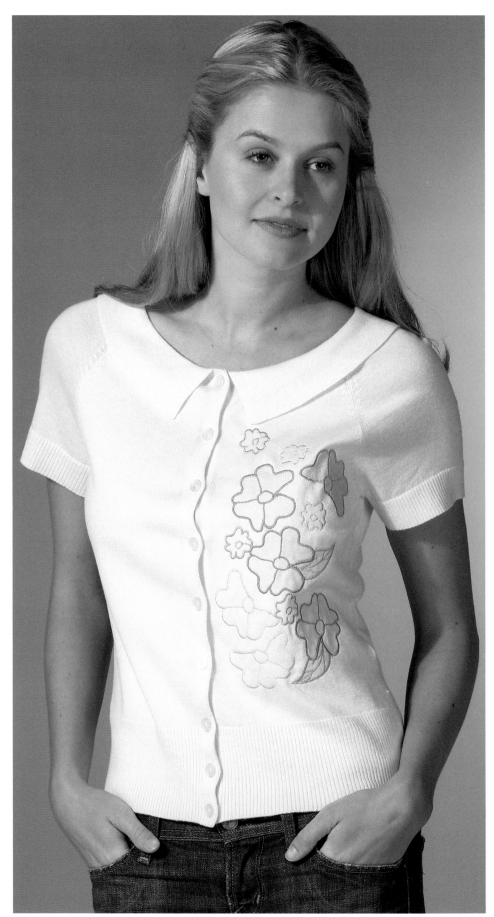

A delicate sweater calls for delicate embroidery. Appliqué designs that are filled with tulle or nothing at all add just a hint of color to this plain, beige cardigan. An airy, asymmetrical design adds interest to an otherwise boring sweater. And this technique is fast; you'll finish it in 90 minutes! Now that's fast fashion!

Plan the Design

1. Even though the embroidery will be applied to only one side, fuse tricot knit interfacing to both the left and right sections. Tricot knit interfacing is one-way directional stretch interfacing. If you want to eliminate the stretch of the garment, apply the interfacing so the interfacing stretch is perpendicular to the stretch of the garment.

2. Try on the garment and stand in front of a mirror to determine the most flattering position for a design area.

3. Audition the templates on the cardigan. An asymmetrical placement creates a vertical line on any figure. Place the templates close to the center front opening and not centered on the left bodice. Pay special attention to any templates that are near the bust point. Move those templates to a more flattering position.

4. Remove the garment carefully.

5. Slide target stickers under each template.

6. Mark the design number and "MI" (for mirror-image, if necessary) on each target sticker.

Embroider the Cardigan

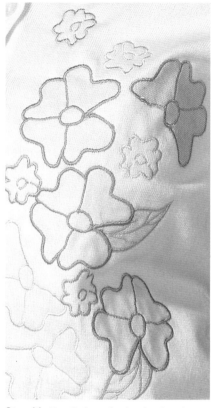

1. Hoop polymesh stabilizer in a large hoop, if available, and spray the stabilizer with temporary adhesive.

2. Position one cardigan front on the stabilizer, capturing as many target stickers as possible in the sewing field. Smooth the sweater onto the sticky stabilizer.

3. Attach the hoop to the machine and position the needle over the first target sticker.

4. Remove the target sticker and sew the first color segment.

5. Lay a piece of pink tulle over the placement guide, and sew the second color segment, the tack-down.

6. Carefully remove the hoop from the machine, but do not remove the fabric from the hoop.

7. Trim the excess tulle and place the hoop back on the machine.

8. Complete the embroidery design.

9. Position the needle over the next closest target sticker.

10. Remove the target sticker. Notice that some of the appliqué designs are completed without the addition of appliqué fabric. Use your discretion on adding and eliminating the tulle.

11. Complete all the embroidery designs.

12. Trim all thread tails and the excess polymesh stabilizer.

Step 11: *Detail of completed embroidery design area.*

Wear with:
- jeans for casual
- swingy skirt for dressy
- black pants for the office

Embellished Jeans

Comfy blue jeans ... dark color is slimming

Materials

- Bell-bottom jeans
- Fusible polymesh stabilizer
- Seam ripper
- 5" x 7" scrap Ultrasuede
- Metafil needle
- Temporary spray adhesive
- Target stickers
- Basic machine embroidery and sewing notions
- MEF6, MEF8, MEF9, MEF22 and MEF23 embroidery designs and templates

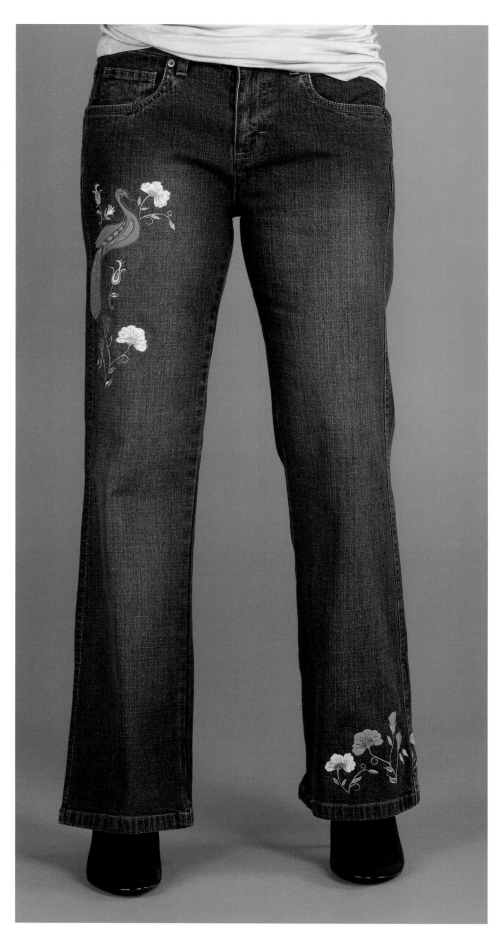

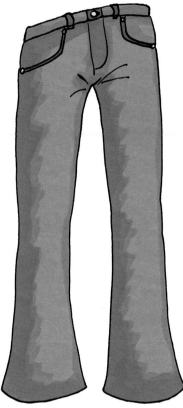

Enhance the vertical line of trendy blue jeans with asymmetrical embroidery on the thigh and opposite hem. Pay careful attention to the placement of the embroidery on the thigh. If it's stitched too close to the side seam it can widen the girth of the thigh. Placed too close to the inseam, the embroidery draws too much attention to the crotch area. Take your time, as detailed in steps one and two of the instructions and you will end up with a fabulously flattering look!

Plan the Right Thigh Design

1. Try on the jeans and stand in front of a mirror to determine the most flattering position for the design area.

2. Audition the templates on the thigh of the jeans. Start by placing the templates on the center of the thigh and then moving just off-center towards the side seam. It might help to step away from the mirror each time you move the template. Walking back into the mirror gives you a fresh view, just like refreshing your computer screen when surfing the Web.

3. Slide a target sticker under each template once you're satisfied with the placement and remove the templates.

Secrets to Success ...

❧ asymmetrical layout

❧ precise placement on the thigh

❧ balanced color

Embroider the Right Thigh Area

1. Use a seam ripper to open the in-seam of the jeans. Start just below the crotch and continue down the seam until the design area (the location of the target stickers) lays flat.

2. Fuse the polymesh stabilizer to the wrong side of the design area.

3. Select a medium-size hoop (5" x 7") and center the design area in the hoop.

4. Position the needle over the first target sticker, design MEF6.

5. Remove the sticker and embroider the first color, the placement guide.

6. Place a scrap of Ultrasuede fabric over the outline and embroider the second color, the tack down.

7. Remove the hoop from the machine carefully, but do not remove the fabric from the hoop.

8. Trim the excess appliqué fabric, cutting as close as possible to the stitching line.

9. Return the hoop to the machine and complete the design.

10. Advance the needle to the second target sticker and embroider the design.

11. Continue embroidering the designs, as in steps 4 through 9, re-hooping as necessary.

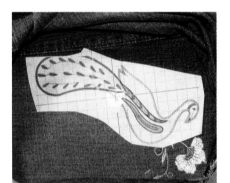

Step 3: *Center design area in medium-size hoop.*

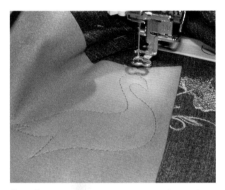

Step 6: *Place Ultrasuede over the outline and embroider.*

Plan the Left Hem Design

1. Place templates of designs MEF8, MEF9 and MEF23 on the hem area.

2. Start at the center front of the leg and continue around the leg towards the side seam.

3. Slide target stickers under each template, mark the design number on each one and remove templates.

Step 1: *Position templates at the hem.*

Step 3: *Use target stickers to mark the design area and remove the templates.*

Embroider the Left Hem

1. Open 5" of the hem at the inseam. Open the inseam to the knee.

2. Hoop polymesh stabilizer and spray it with temporary adhesive.

3. Center the hem on the stabilizer.

4. Pin the leg to the stabilizer near the perimeter of the hoop.

5. Attach the hoop to the machine and position the needle over the first target sticker.

6. Remove the target sticker and embroider the design.

7. Position the needle over the next closest target sticker and repeat the process.

8. Embroider all of the designs.

9. Remove the pants from the hoop.

10. Trim the polymesh stabilizer.

11. Sew the inseam and the hem.

Step 4: *Pin the jean leg to the stabilizer near the hoop perimeter.*

Step 10: *Once the design is complete, there will be a considerable amount of stabilizer in need of trimming.*

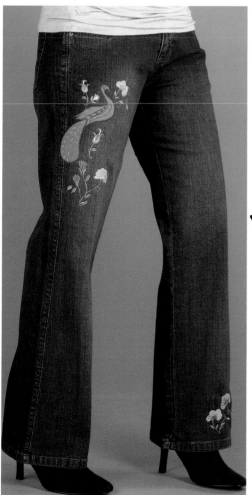

Wear with:

- stretchy knit top
- coral and turquoise jewelry
- boots

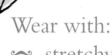

Blue Jacket

Light and airy Boho designs make this project a breeze

Materials

- Cotton jacket with cuff and patch pockets
- Polymesh stabilizer
- Tape
- Seam ripper
- Centering rulers
- Temporary spray adhesive
- Target stickers
- Basic machine embroidery and sewing notions
- MEF18, MEF19, MEF24 and MEF25 embroidery designs and templates

There are four key areas of embellishment on this blue jacket: the bodice, pocket, collar and cuffs. In this chapter, we'll focus on the bodice embellishment. The bodice embellishment accomplishes two things. It creates a vertical line and it links the pocket, collar and cuff embroidery. Without the bodice embroidery, the overall design of the jacket would fail because the cuff and pocket embroidery create a horizontal line at the hip and the collar embroidery is too delicate to stand alone.

Plan the Jacket Front Design

1. Lay the jacket on a flat surface with all buttons closed, except for the top button. Open the collar so it falls open naturally.

2. Start placing the templates on the left front, high on the shoulder. Make sure the embroidery design falls close to the collar but is not obstructed by the open collar.

3. Continue placing the templates to create an almost continuous line of embroidery around the collar and down the left front. Place the designs close to the front placket.

4. Lay two or three templates around the collar on the right side.

5. Put the jacket on and stand in front of a mirror. Make any necessary adjustments to the design areas.

6. Remove the jacket carefully.

7. Slide target stickers under each template, mark the design name on each one and remove the templates.

Step 4: *Position the templates down the front, around the collar and on the collar.*

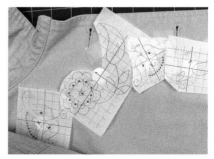

Step 7: *Slide template stickers under each template.*

Embroider the Jacket Front

1. Hoop polymesh stabilizer and the jacket, centering the target sticker up near the shoulder. It may help to turn the sleeve inside out while hooping. Make sure only one layer of fabric is secured in the hoop.

2. Attach the hoop to the machine and position the needle over the target sticker.

3. Remove the target sticker and embroider the first design.

4. Continue embroidering the design area, re-hooping as necessary.

5. Embroider near the center front by hooping a layer of polymesh stabilizer, spraying it with temporary adhesive and pinning the jacket to the stabilizer.

Embroider the Collar

1. Place the MEF24 template on the point of the collar and tape it to the collar.

2. Hoop polymesh stabilizer. If you're using a medium or large hoop, you can embroider both collar points in one hooping.

3. Tape and pin the collar point to the stabilizer, allowing room for the second collar point.

4. Attach the hoop to the machine and position the needle over the template.

5. Remove the template and embroider the design.

6. Remove the hoop from the machine.

7. Tape and pin the second collar point to the stabilizer.

8. Repeat steps 4 through 6 on the second collar.

9. Trim the excess stabilizer.

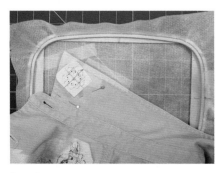

Step 3: *Tape and pin the collar point to the hooped stabilizer.*

Step 5: *Embroider the collar design.*

Step 7: *Tape and pin the other collar point to the stabilizer.*

Embroider the Cuff

1. Measure the width of the cuff from the buttonhole to the button and the height from topstitching to topstitching. These measurements will determine the size of the embroidery designs.

2. Size the selected designs in embroidery software to fit the cuff. I increased MEF19 to fit in half of the 8½" x 3½" cuff. MEF19 now measures 4" x 3".

3. Print two templates of the enlarged design.

4. Fold the cuff in half and place it on a flat surface.

5. Center the template on the cuff, positioning one edge of the design right next to the button. If you measured correctly, the opposite end of the design should reach the fold.

6. Slide a target sticker under the template.

7. Turn the sleeve inside out.

8. Hoop polymesh stabilizer and spray with temporary adhesive.

9. Place the cuff in the hoop, adding pins for extra security. Most likely the whole cuff will not lie flat in the hoop. Smooth the sleeve as much as possible.

10. Attach the hoop to the machine and position the needle over the target sticker.

11. Remove the template.

12. Distribute the weight of the jacket on the table around the machine; don't let it slide off the table. Stay with the machine when embroidering to make sure the foot doesn't get caught in the sleeve.

13. Embroider the design.

14. Remove the hoop from the machine and the cuff from the stabilizer.

15. Place the cuff on a flat work surface and position the template on the cuff. Make sure the template design connects with the embroidered design.

16. Slide a target sticker under the template and remove the template.

17. Repeat steps 7 through 13 for embroidering the second design.

18. Mirror-image the design for the opposite cuff and repeat all steps.

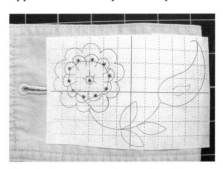

Step 5: *Center the template on the cuff.*

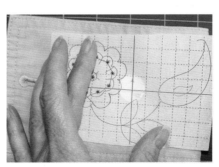

Step 6: *Slide a target sticker in place.*

Step 9: *Place the cuff in the hoop.*

Step 12: *Stay near the machine as the design is embroidered.*

Step 16: *Slide a target sticker under the template.*

Easy-Finish Color Sequencing

Turn a seven-color design into a three-color design and speed up your finishing time. Examine the embroidery design in customizing software. Change the color of each segment to cut down on thread changes. Play with the thread color until you're satisfied with the finished results. No need to save the changes in software, you can make all these changes at the machines but do write down your changes. This will help you remember in case you get interrupted during the embroidery process.

MEF19 Changed Color Sequence

1. Brown
2. Medium Brown
3. Medium Brown
4. Brown
5. Brown
6. Beige
7. Beige

Original Color Sequence

1. Brown
2. Beige
3. Tan
4. White
5. Black
6. Rust
7. Cocoa

Plan the Pocket Design

1. Open a new file in customizing software and select a large hoop.

2. Copy and paste MEF18 and MEF19 into the hoop (Figure 5-1).

3. Add MEF24 and MEF25. Copy and paste a few repeats of MEF24 and MEF25, linking the designs to one another (Figure 5-2).

4. Save the design as Pocket1 and print a template of it.

5. Place the Pocket1 template on the jacket.

6. Slide a target sticker under the crosshair and remove the template.

7. Use a ruler and removable marker (chalk) to extend the crosshair. Draw the lines beyond the pocket area.

8. Use a seam ripper to remove the pocket. Set aside the pocket.

9. Use two rulers to connect the lines on the jacket.

10. Place a target sticker on the intersection of the rulers. If a button poses a threat to the embroidery process, remove it and sew it back on later.

Figure 5-1

Figure 5-2

Step 5: *Place template on the jacket pocket.*

Step 9: *Connect the lines, using two rulers.*

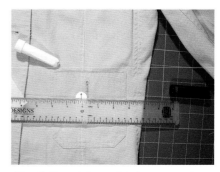

Step 7: *Extend the crosshair by using a ruler and marking with chalk.*

When a patch pocket lays smack in the middle of a desirable design area, don't fret. You can stitch right over it without losing the use of the pocket. With a little planning and some ingenuity, you'll have a smashing outfit. The key is to select open, airy designs that connect easily and plan the project carefully. I learned this interesting technique from Maureen Egan, a contributing editor for "Designs in Machine Embroidery."

Embroider the Pocket

1. Hoop polymesh stabilizer and spray it with temporary adhesive.

2. Position the jacket on the stabilizer and pin it in place for extra security.

3. Attach the hoop to the machine and position the needle over the crosshair.

4. Remove the target sticker.

5. Travel through the design to avoid stitching the portion that will be hidden by the pocket.

6. Embroider all colors that extend beyond the pocket area.

7. Remove the jacket from the hoop and trim the stabilizer.

8. Place the pocket on the jacket to check the embroidery.

9. Open the seam allowances of the pocket and press them flat.

10. Hoop polymesh stabilizer and spray it with temporary adhesive.

11. Center the pocket on the stabilizer and finger-press the pocket to the adhesive stabilizer, adding pins if necessary.

12. Position the needle over the target sticker.

13. Embroider the portion of the design that will stitch on the pocket, allowing the excess to stitch onto the stabilizer only.

14. Use the template for a reference guide. When in doubt about a certain portion, stitch it anyway.

15. Remove the hoop from the machine and release the stabilizer from the hoop.

16. Trim the stabilizer close to the stitches.

17. Fold the seam allowances to the back and press.

18. Pin the pocket on the jacket, carefully aligning the embroidery designs.

19. Sew the pocket in place.

Step 5: *Travel through the design.*

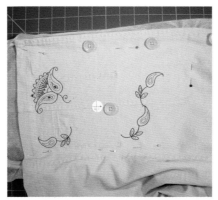

Step 6: *Embroider all colors that go beyond the pocket area.*

Step 8: *Check the embroidery by placing the pocket on the jacket.*

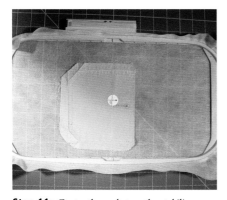

Step 11: *Center the pocket on the stabilizer.*

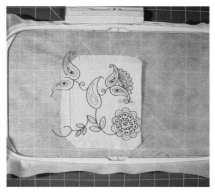

Step 13: *Embroider the pocket design.*

Step 17: *Fold the seam allowances back.*

Wear with:
- comfy blue jeans or a brown skirt
- boots
- leather belt and bag

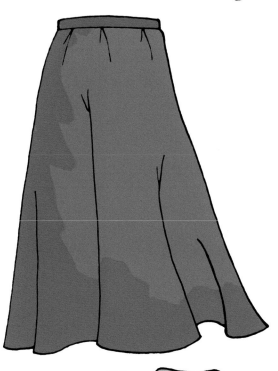

Tweed Suit

Love the power of the flower

Materials

- Tweed suit
- 6 assorted colors 4" scraps hand-dyed wool felt
- Polymesh stabilizer
- Seam ripper
- Appliqué scissors
- Temporary spray adhesive
- Target stickers
- Basic machine embroidery and sewing notions
- MEF28, MEF29 and MEF30 embroidery designs and templates

Even though embroidering on tweed suiting is trendy and fashionable, it does present some challenges for the embroiderer. Tweed is nubby, so care must be taken when selecting embroidery designs. If the design features a heavy fill-stitch, the nubbiness could shadow through the embroidery thread, or at the very least, present a dimpled surface. Thread color is also a concern. Since tweed is a weave of contrasting fibers, it can be difficult to choose an embroidery thread that will separate itself from the tweed. The tweed in the photo is a gorgeous pink but when examined closely, many colors and values are present in the weave: everything from a pale pink to a bold burgundy with a splash of yellow and orange.

One solution to these challenges is machine appliqué. The large expanse of an appliqué fabric will cover the textured tweed while providing a powerful punch of color. The three appliqué designs—MEF28, MEF29 and MEF30—feature a buttonhole stitch as the outline and the trimmed fabric will be visible beyond the stitching. Unlike the smooth finish of satin-edge appliqué designs, it's a style that complements a nubby tweed quite well.

Plan the Design

1. Put the jacket on and stand in front of a mirror. Audition the templates on the left front bodice. Once you're satisfied with the placement, pin or tape the templates to the jacket.

2. Take the jacket off and slide target stickers under each template. Mark the stickers with the appropriate design number.

Step 2: *Slide target stickers under each template.*

Embroider the Suit

Detail of embroidered design.

1. Separate the facing from its lining with a seam ripper. Open enough of the seam so you can access the front bodice and hoop without catching the lining.

2. Hoop polymesh stabilizer and spray it with temporary adhesive.

3. Smooth the bodice onto the sticky stabilizer, centering as many target stickers as possible in the hoop.

4. Position the needle over the target sticker closest to the neck and select design MEF28.

5. Stitch the first color segment, the placement guide.

6. Place one 4" square of the hand-dyed wool felt over the placement guide.

7. Sew the second color segment.

8. Remove the hoop carefully from the machine (<u>but not the fabric from the hoop</u>) and trim away the excess fabric. Use appliqué scissors to avoid snipping the tweed.

9. Place the hoop back on the machine and stitch color segment three.

10. Repeat for all six flowers.

11. Trim any excess polymesh stabilizer from the wrong side of the jacket.

12. Pin the lining back in position and press.

13. Hand-sew the lining closed for the finished look shown.

The Challenges of Tweed

❧ lots of contrasting fibers

❧ loose weave

❧ textured surface

Appliqué is the answer! Hand-dyed wool felt adds punch

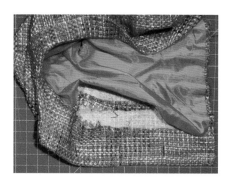

Step 1: *Use a seam ripper to separate the lining and the facing.*

Step 8: *Use a scissors to carefully trim excess fabric from the embroidered design.*

TIP

Don't be afraid to use a small hoop and re-hoop for each flower in this project. When working with a jacket that has had the lining separated, it can be quite awkward to get the fabric to flatten in a medium or large hoop.

Wear with:
- a stylish briefcase
- pumps
- no jewelry
- a smile!

Chapter 3

Notable Necklines

Steps to Success . . .

- Examine the garment and look for a focal point. Possibilities include embroidering at the edge of the neckline, the yoke area or surrounding the neckline finish (ribbing).
- Make sure the collar points will not hide the embroidery.
- Choose a stabilizer that will hold the neckline in the hoop. Adhesive cut-away, wash-away or tear-away stabilizers work best, but a combination of temporary spray adhesive, pins and cut-away works very well.

Start with the Basics . . .

Brown Corduroy
Jacket

Sheer Organdy
Blouse

Red Pullover

Red Pullover

*Try pearls,
crystals or metal
studs to add that
special sparkle*

Materials

- Cotton sweater knit pullover
- Tricot knit interfacing
- Polymesh stabilizer
- Stretch needle size 80
- Hot fix pearls
- Hot fix silver studs
- Hot fix tool
- Temporary spray adhesive
- 24 target stickers
- Basic machine embroidery and sewing notions
- MEF27 embroidery design

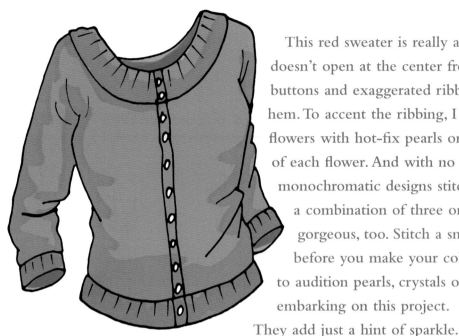

This red sweater is really a mock cardigan, since it doesn't open at the center front. I loved the sweet pearl buttons and exaggerated ribbing at the neckline and hem. To accent the ribbing, I added small monochromatic flowers with hot-fix pearls or silver studs in the center of each flower. And with no thread changes, these monochromatic designs stitched up in a hurry. Of course, a combination of three or more colors would look gorgeous, too. Stitch a small flower on a similar fabric before you make your color decision. Don't forget to audition pearls, crystals or studs before embarking on this project. They add just a hint of sparkle.

Plan the Design

1. Fuse tricot knit interfacing to the wrong side of the sweater front. Normally, the stretch of the interfacing is fused in the opposite direction of the sweater's stretch, but in this sample, I fused the interfacing with the stretch in the same direction as the sweater since it's tight-fitting and I didn't want to eliminate all of the stretch.

2. Put the sweater on and stand in front of a full-length mirror.

3. Use target stickers to designate the position of each flower, MEF27, instead of printing templates of the tiny flower. The sticker and flower are approximately the same size, so place the stickers on the sweater, starting at the center front of the ribbed collar. Keep adding stickers until the collar is framed.

4. Continue adding stickers down the center front, bordering the buttons.

5. Remove the garment carefully when satisfied with the number of stickers and turn it inside out.

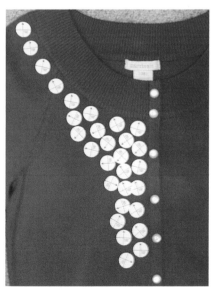

Step 4: *Place target stickers down the center front where each flower design will land.*

Embroider the Sweater

1. Hoop polymesh stabilizer and spray it generously with temporary adhesive.

2. Place the collar area on the hoop and smooth the garment to the sticky stabilizer. Make sure all wrinkles or bubbles are removed, as it's very important for the stretchy sweater to lay flat in the hoop.

Step 9: *Move from one target sticker to the next to embroider each design, lifting the water-soluble stabilizer and removing each sticker before embroidering.*

3. Pin the garment to the stabilizer near the perimeter of the hoop.

4. Attach the hoop to the machine, position the needle over a target sticker and then remove the target sticker.

5. Place a piece of water-soluble stabilizer over the design area and embroider the design.

6. Position the needle over the next closest target sticker.

7. Lift the water-soluble stabilizer and remove the target sticker.

8. Embroider the design.

9. Continue in this manner until you have embroidered all of the designs in the hoop.

10. Remove the stabilizer and garment from the hoop.

11. Trim the excess stabilizer from the wrong side.

12. Hoop a new piece of polymesh stabilizer and spray it with adhesive.

13. Place the opposite collar area on the hoop and repeat steps 2 through 11 for this opposite side.

14. Hoop a third piece of polymesh stabilizer once the entire collar is embroidered, center the center-front section in the hoop and embroider. With a 5" x 7" hoop, the center front can be embroidered in one hooping.

15. Remove the garment from the hoop and place it on a protective surface.

Embellish the Embroidery

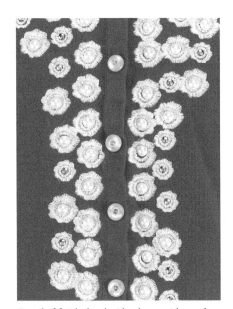

Detail of finished embroidered area with metal nail heads and pearls attached.

1. Use tweezers to place one metal nail head or pearl in the center of a flower.

2. Apply the hot, flat tip to the nail head or pearl and lift it up.

3. Wait for the glue to bubble, and then touch the nail head or pearl to the desired location. Hold in position for 20 seconds. Touch the nail head with your finger to make sure it is permanently attached.

4. Repeat steps 1 through 3 for all remaining flower centers for the finished look shown.

Wear with:
- a white skirt
- red pumps
- pearl earrings
- big sunglasses

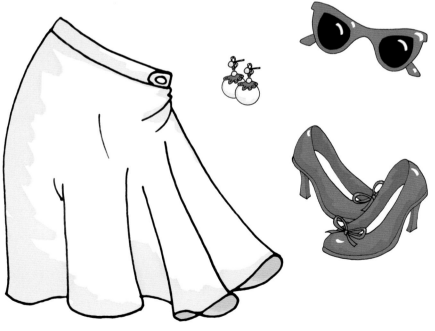

Brown Corduroy Jacket

A fresh combo … corduroy the color of chocolate, enriched with baby-blue flowers

Materials

- Brown stretch corduroy jacket, center front opening with yoke
- Polymesh stabilizer
- 2 yd. narrow trim
- Stretch needle
- Monofilament thread
- Large hoop, if available
- Stretch needle size 80
- Open toe foot
- Temporary spray adhesive
- Target stickers
- Basic machine embroidery and sewing notions
- MEF9 and MEF23 embroidery designs and templates

Embroidered yokes are flattering on all feminine figures—from small-busted to the well-endowed. The key is in the placement. Well-endowed figures do better with embroidery away from the bust. Instead, keep it up near the face, drawing the eye to your smile. Embroidery scattered across the yoke, ending above the bust point on smaller figures adds interest in an area that lacks shape. All figures should avoid embroidery right on the bust point unless the entire expanse of fabric is embroidered in a continuous vertical or horizontal line of embroidery.

This brown jacket has beautiful lines and details that are hidden by its deep brown shade. The embroidery on the yoke brings the viewer's eyes to the face and reveals the yoke detail. The tiny trim, applied with monofilament thread, further enhances the yoke. The same trim is added to the sleeve cuffs.

Light blue and dark brown seems like a very trendy color combination, but it's been around forever. Think soft-washed blue jeans and brown cowboy boots or the twinkle of a robin's egg hidden in a cozy nest.

Embroidering on corduroy is challenging. The width of the wale and the depth of the pile can make or break a beautiful embroidery design. The narrower the space between the wales, the better your chances of success. Select designs without delicate outlines that can get lost in the corduroy. A topper, usually water-soluble stabilizer, is required to keep the stitches from sinking into the lofty fabric. Testing on a scrap of corduroy is a worthwhile endeavor; you may find an adjustment to the stitch density is required.

Plan the Design

Step 2: *Try out the design with templates.*

1. Try the jacket on and button the front closed. Leave one or two buttons undone at the neck if this is how you would normally wear the garment.

2. Audition the templates on the jacket. Make sure the collar points will not obstruct the embroidery.

3. Check the overall placement of the embroidery. Is it flattering or drawing too much attention to the bust line?

Consider adding the embellishment higher in the yoke area. It doesn't have to sit on the yoke seam. Make any necessary adjustments.

4. Take the jacket off.

5. Replace the templates with target stickers and mark the design name and instructions on each sticker.

Embroider the Jacket

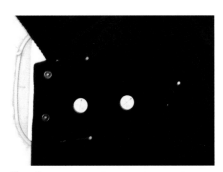

Step 3: *Position the jacket on the hooped stabilizer.*

The finished embroidered yoke and trim.

1. Hoop polymesh stabilizer in a large hoop and spray it with temporary spray adhesive. If a large hoop is not available, use a standard 4" square hoop and re-hoop for the second embroidery design.

2. Turn the jacket inside out so that it will lay flat in the hoop. Doing this also eliminates the chance of stitching the sleeve to the garment front.

3. Position the left yoke on the stabilizer and press it to the tacky surface. If possible, pull the facing out from under the jacket front. If buttonholes or snaps don't permit this, pin the facing to the garment to keep the two layers together as one.

4. Pin the yoke to the stabilizer for extra security.

5. Attach the hoop to the machine and position the needle over the first target sticker.

6. Remove the target sticker.

7. Add a piece of water-soluble stabilizer over the design area and embroider the design.

8. Position the needle over the second target sticker and complete the embroidery.

9. Remove the stabilizer and jacket from the hoop.

10. Repeat steps 2 through 8 on the right yoke, mirror-imaging the design before embroidering it.

11. Trim all excess polymesh stabilizer and tear away the water-soluble stabilizer.

12. Select a narrow zigzag (SW: 1.7; SL: 1.6) and attach an open toe foot.

13. Thread the needle with monofilament thread and the bobbin with regular sewing thread to match the fabric.

14. Turn under ¼" on one end of the trim and pin that end to the collar where it meets the collar stand. Couch over the trim, guiding the trim as you sew.

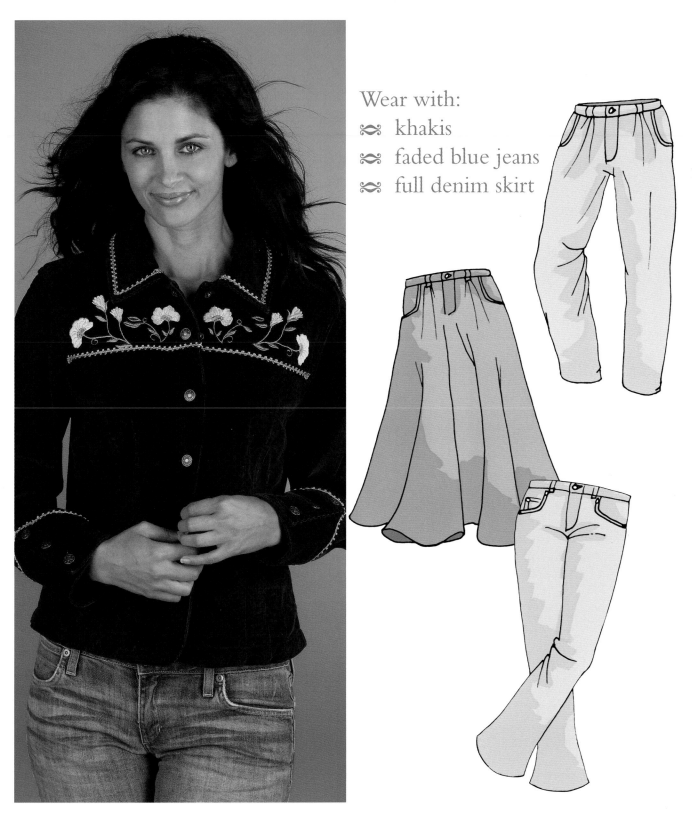

Wear with:
- khakis
- faded blue jeans
- full denim skirt

Sheer Organdy Blouse

For a day in the city ... white keeps you cool, black adds fabulous sophistication

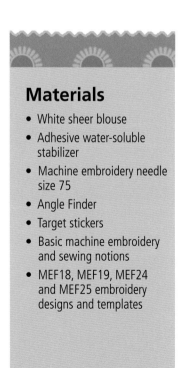

Materials

- White sheer blouse
- Adhesive water-soluble stabilizer
- Machine embroidery needle size 75
- Angle Finder
- Target stickers
- Basic machine embroidery and sewing notions
- MEF18, MEF19, MEF24 and MEF25 embroidery designs and templates

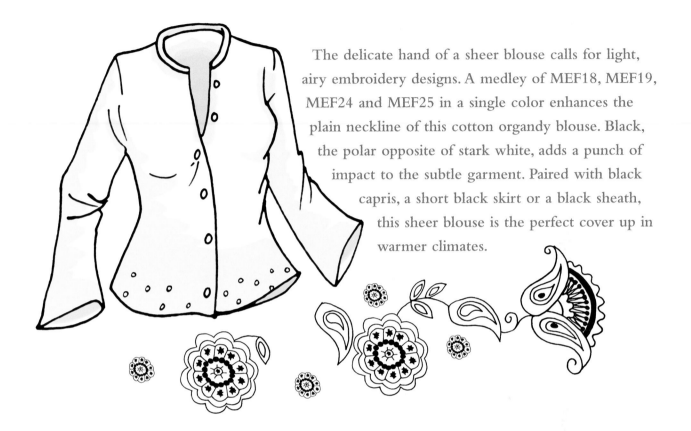

The delicate hand of a sheer blouse calls for light, airy embroidery designs. A medley of MEF18, MEF19, MEF24 and MEF25 in a single color enhances the plain neckline of this cotton organdy blouse. Black, the polar opposite of stark white, adds a punch of impact to the subtle garment. Paired with black capris, a short black skirt or a black sheath, this sheer blouse is the perfect cover up in warmer climates.

Plan the Design

1. Try on the blouse and stand in front of a mirror.

2. Audition the templates on the blouse, taping them in position as you work on the composition. Make sure the templates are placed close to the neck edge to draw the focus to your face. I opted for symmetrical placement on this garment.

3. Remove the blouse.

4. Slide target stickers under the templates and remove the templates.

TIP

Since cotton organdy is a strong fabric and the chosen designs have a low stitch count, only a minimum of stabilizer is needed. Use one that is completely removable because you do not want the stabilizer to show through the transparent fabric. I used an adhesive water-soluble stabilizer. It held the fabric during the embroidery process and then simply washed away.

Embroider the Blouse

1. Cut a piece of adhesive water-soluble stabilizer large enough to cover the bottom of the hoop.

2. Remove the protective plastic shield and finger-press the sticky surface to the bottom of the hoop.

3. Place the blouse on the sticky stabilizer, centering the center front edge.

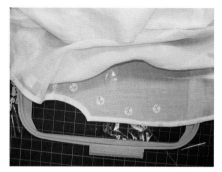

Step 3: *Center the blouse on the sticky stabilizer.*

4. Position the needle over the first target sticker and remove the target sticker.

5. Embroider the design and then position the needle over the next closest target sticker.

6. Use the Angle Finder if rotation is required. Refer to Angle Finder, page 24, if more information on use is needed. Center the Angle Finder on the target sticker, keeping the straight edge of the Angle Finder parallel with the hoop's straight edge and the zero degree mark at the top of the hoop.

7. Spin the dial on the Angle Finder until the red arrow lines up with the target sticker's black arrow.

8. Note the designated degrees of rotation and rotate the design on the machine screen.

9. Embroider design.

10. Repeat steps 6 through 9 until all of the designs are stitched in the hoop.

11. Remove the stabilizer from the hoop and carefully trim away the excess stabilizer.

12. Attach a new piece of sticky stabilizer to the wrong side of the hoop and repeat the process above.

13. Repeat steps 1 through 12 on the second side of the blouse front, being sure to mirror-image all of the designs for a symmetrical duplication.

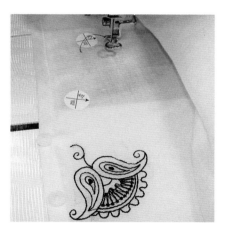

Step 5: *Embroider the first design and move to the next target sticker.*

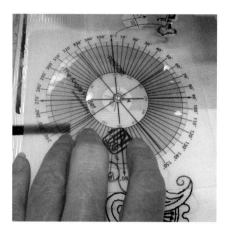

Step 6: *Use the Angle Finder to rotate the second design.*

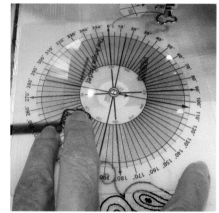

Step 7: *Line up the red arrow on the Angle Finder with the black arrow on the target sticker.*

Wear with:

- a stretchy tank
- wedge espadrilles
- a Boho bag

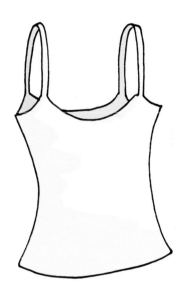

Chapter 4 Classy Collars and Cuffs

Steps to Success . . .

- Maintain the roll of a collar when embroidering those without neck bands.
- Center a single design in the collar point.
- Embroider both collar points, and then work your way toward the center back of the neck.
- Don't let the cuff embroidery overpower other embroidered elements on the garment.
- Select designs that are fairly low in stitch count, as dense designs don't allow the cuff to flow.
- Release the hem of a cuff so you're stitching on only one fabric layer, but always design the cuff embroidery before releasing any hems.

Start with the Basics . . .

Capri pants

Jeans

Silk Blouse

Floral Jeans

Sprinkle some delicate flowers along the curve of the pocket

Materials

- Blue jeans
- Polymesh stabilizer
- Tear-away stabilizer
- Pins
- Seam ripper
- Temporary spray adhesive
- Target stickers
- Basic machine embroidery and sewing notions
- MEF11, MEF13, MEF14 and MEF15 embroidery designs and templates

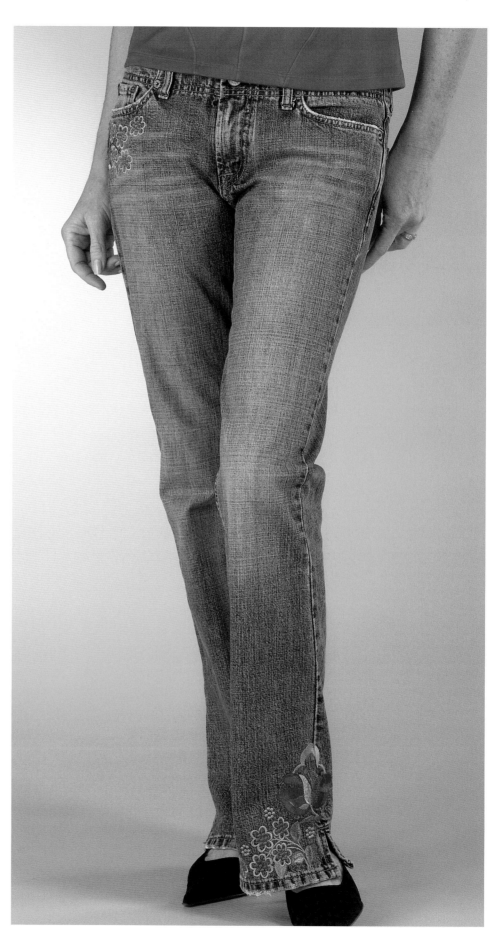

What's old is new again! Fashion jeans embroidered at the pocket and hemline are something many of us wore in the '60s and '70s. The fad is back and here to stay. Embroidered jeans can be found in high-priced boutiques for $150 or more. But you can create your own floral signature for a fraction of the cost! Start with a pair of great-fitting jeans and make sure the length is where you want it because once you add embroidery at the hem, shortening or lengthening the leg is no longer an option. Embroidery at the hem of a pant leg is flattering on every figure. If you're pear-shaped, boot-cut jeans with embroidery can help balance your figure while embroidered bell-bottoms look best on ladies with long legs and even proportions. Plus-size figures look fashionable in embroidered palazzos. So whatever your shape, scatter a little embroidery at the hem and the pocket, and you'll add a little kick to your step!

Plan the Left Hem Design

1. Audition the templates on the pant leg. Since these jeans have a notched seam, I used it as a focal point for the designs but not the true center of the overall design. I wanted more than one-third of the embroidery to be visible from the front.

2. Tape the templates on the jeans and try on the jeans. Stand in front of a mirror to determine if you like the placement. Remember, the length of the pant leg cannot be changed after the embroidery process. Make any necessary changes now.

3. Take off the jeans carefully.

Embroider the Left Hem

1. Use a seam ripper to open the inside seam of the jeans about 12". This is a tricky situation; you must open the leg far enough so it lays flat in the hoop but not so high that you can't sew the seam closed if you have to topstitch. Be careful and open the seam a few inches at a time, checking to see if you've opened enough of the seam to access the design area.

2. Turn the jeans inside out.

Step 5: *Open the pant leg and lay the design area flat on the hoop.*

3. Hoop polymesh stabilizer and spray it with temporary adhesive.

4. Place the hem on the stabilizer parallel to the edge of the hoop to make sure the leg is straight.

5. Open the pant leg to access the design area and pin the design area. Use the templates as a guide for how much of the pant leg must lay flat. Make sure the jeans are open enough so the embroidery foot can reach all of the design area.

6. Slide target stickers under the templates, remove the templates and write the sequence number on each target sticker and MI if mirror-imaging is required.

7. Attach the hoop to the machine and position the needle over the first target sticker. Wrap the bulk of the jeans around the bed of the machine to evenly distribute the weight of the jeans.

8. Remove the target sticker and embroider the first design, watching the embroidery foot as it travels across the jeans.

9. Hold down the top of the pant leg to avoid getting the excess fabric caught in the embroidery foot.

10. Position the needle over the second target sticker and embroider the design.

11. Repeat for the third design.

12. Remove the hoop from the machine and release the stabilizer from the hoop.

13. Trim the stabilizer from the wrong side, making sure you eliminate the stabilizer behind the slit.

14. Trim all thread tails.

15. Sew the inseam closed.

Step 6: *Slide target stickers under the templates.*

Step 13: *Trim the stabilizer.*

Step 14: *Trim all thread tails.*

Plan the Front Pocket Design

1. Lay the jeans on a flat surface and tape template MEF14 and MEF15 just below the pocket.

2. Try the jeans on with the templates in place. Make any necessary adjustments and remove the jeans.

3. Unbutton and unzip the jeans and then turn them inside out to examine the pocket (A).

If the side seam is not flat-felled, open the side seam with a seam ripper (B).

Lift the pocket up and pin it to the waistband, keeping the front of the jeans flat (C).

4. Slide target stickers under the templates and remove the templates.

Step 3A: *Examine the pocket.*

Step 3B: *Open the side seam with a seam ripper.*

Step 3C: *Be sure to keep the front of the jeans flat when you pin the pocket to the waistband.*

Embroider the Front Pocket

1. Hoop polymesh stabilizer and spray it with temporary adhesive.

2. Finger-press the pocket front area of the jeans onto the stabilizer.

3. Open the jeans to expose the design area. Make sure only one layer of the jeans are in the hoop.

4. Pin the jeans to the stabilizer.

5. Place the Angle Finder on the target sticker to determine the required rotation for the design.

6. Rotate the design on the machine.

7. Attach the hoop to the machine and wrap the legs around the bed of the machine. Do not let the legs drag off the edge of the table.

8. Position the needle over the target sticker and embroider the design.

9. Remove the hoop from the machine and the jeans from the hoop.

10. Trim the excess stabilizer.

11. Sew the side seam closed catching the pocket in the seam.

Step 4: *Pin the jeans to the stabilizer.*

Step 5: *Use Angle Finder to determine the necessary rotation.*

Step 7: *Attach the hoop to the machine, taking care with the legs, so they don't pull on the design while embroidering.*

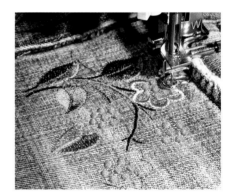

Step 8: *Embroider the design.*

Wear with:
- a crop jacket
- a tucked-in cami
- a crinkly belt
- pointy high heels

Capri Pants

So summery! Embroidered cuffs draw the eye down and balance wide hips

Materials

- Capri pants with cuffs
- Polymesh stabilizer
- Temporary spray adhesive
- Target stickers
- Basic machine embroidery and sewing notions
- MEF21 embroidery design and template

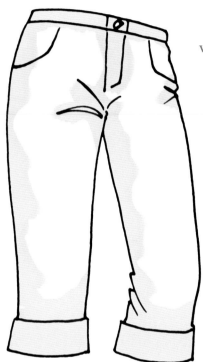

Summertime, summertime. What better way to herald in the warm, colorful days of summer than with capri pants? Although many of you said goodbye to short shorts a long time ago, you probably still wear capri pants. These short pants give you the same carefree feeling with an extra measure of modesty. But modesty doesn't have to be boring. Add a little splash of color at the cuff for a fun and funky look.

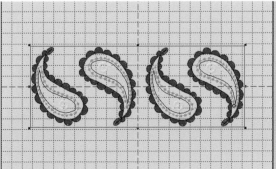

Plan the Design

1. Measure the cuff horizontally and vertically. Use the measurement to size the embroidery border.

2. Open MEF21 in customizing software (Figure 4-1). Travel through the design and delete color #2.

3. Select a large horizontal hoop.

4. Copy and paste the design three times.

5. Move the designs in a horizontal line, mirror-imaging every other one.

6. Use the grid as a guide to make sure the designs are evenly spaced (Figure 4-2).

7. Color sort the designs since none of the designs overlap. Check the size of the border. Shrink or enlarge the design to fit the cuff if the circumference of the leg doesn't divide evenly into the border. Save the design as "Capris Border" in the appropriate format.

8. Print a template of Capris Border.

9. Cut around the template, paper doll-style so you can get a good look at the outer dimensions of the border.

10. Tape the border on the cuff, centering the design under the knee.

11. Add a second template to continue around the leg. You may have to add one repeat of a single paisley design to fill the whole leg.

12. Determine if any final size adjustments are required. Make them now if needed.

13. Slide a target sticker under the template and remove the template.

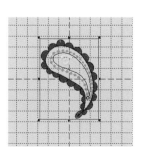

Figure 4-1

Figure 4-2

Embroider the Capris

1. Remove the stitching that holds the cuff in place.

2. Remove the hem stitching so you'll embroider on one layer of fabric.

3. Open the inseam so the cuff area lays flat.

4. Hoop polymesh stabilizer and spray it with temporary adhesive.

5. Finger-press the cuff area to the stabilizer, centering the crosshair. Add pins for extra security.

6. Attach the hoop to the machine and position the needle over the target sticker.

7. Rotate the design if necessary.

8. Remove the target sticker and embroider the design.

9. Remove the hoop from the machine and release the stabilizer.

10. Hoop a second piece of stabilizer and press the remaining area of the cuff onto the stabilizer.

11. Attach the hoop to the machine and position the needle over the target sticker.

12. Remove the target sticker and embroider the design.

13. Mirror the embroidery on the opposite cuff by using a centering ruler to measure the distance from the seam allowance at the inseam to the outside edge of the embroidery. In the sample, the embroidery is 1¼" from the seam allowance.

14. Place the template 1¼" from the seam allowance on the opposite leg.

15. Slide a target sticker under the template and remove the template.

16. Repeat steps 6 through 12 for the finished look shown.

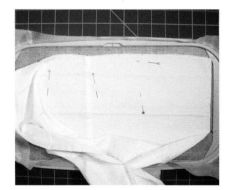

Step 5: *Place the cuff on the stabilizer, pinning for extra hold.*

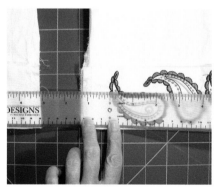

Step 13: *Use a centering ruler to measure the distance from the seam allowance at the inseam to the design's outside edge.*

Step 14: *Place the template based on the outcome of the measurement in step 13.*

TIP

The beauty of using target stickers on cuffs is that the crosshair is highly visible. The crosshair tells you two things: where the center of the design is located and what direction is up. This is very helpful after releasing the cuff from the pant leg. Often, the embroidery has to be stitched "upside down" so it appears "right-side up" when the cuff is sewn back in position. It's easy to confuse the two directions with a hooped item. Use the target stickers faithfully and you'll never doubt your planning again.

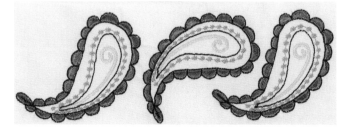

Step 16: *Detail of the finished cuff.*

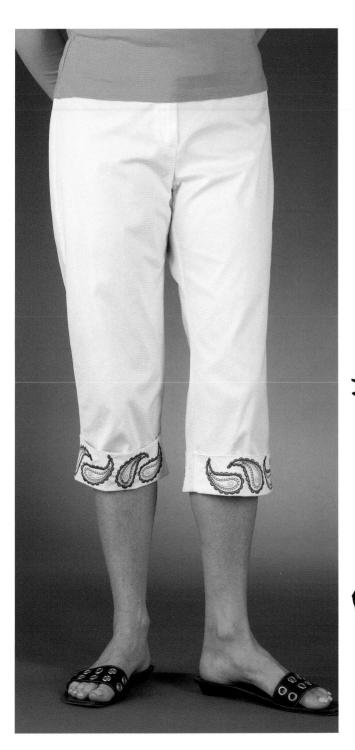

Wear with:

- ∞ an orange T-shirt
- ∞ a straw hat and bag
- ∞ sunglasses
- ∞ flip-flops

Silk Blouse

*Lovely lace
edging is
a luxurious
finishing touch*

Materials

- Silk blouse
- Aqua Melt adhesive-backed water-soluble stabilizer
- 24" x 10" piece tulle, same color as garment
- Water-soluble stabilizer (regular weight, film-type)
- Large hoop (optional)
- Temporary spray adhesive
- Target stickers
- Basic machine embroidery and sewing notions
- MEF16 and MEF17 embroidery designs and templates

I love the off-the-edge embroidery technique. It's one of my favorite ways to apply embroidery to a finished garment. Applying embroidery to the edge of a finished collar presents a few challenges but the impact is worth it. Number one: It's imperative the roll of the collar is not affected by the application of the embroidery. Number two: Since the embroidery will extend off the edge of the collar, it will need a permanent stabilizer to hold the shape of the stitches. Number three: The collar and the open-lace designs are highly visible so the permanent stabilizer must add to the finished look or vanish beyond the stitches.

Prepare the Collar

1. Pin the collar to itself as it hangs on the hanger.

2. Place the opened collar on the tulle, both fabrics right side up, and pin the collar to the tulle, making sure at least 2" of tulle extends beyond the collar edge. The tulle will act as a permanent stabilizer.

Step 1: To maintain the natural roll of the collar, pin it while it hangs.

Step 2: Pin the collar to the tulle.

3. Baste the collar to the tulle.

4. Flip the collar over and trim away the excess tulle under the collar.

5. Select a large hoop, if available, and hoop the Aqua Melt.

6. Score the surface inside the inner hoop.

7. Remove the protective paper, exposing the sticky surface.

8. Position the collar on the stabilizer, making sure the collar corner is in the sewing field.

9. Place template MEF16 on the corner, extending a portion of the design off the collar edge.

10. Tape the template to the collar. If the template is rotated, use the Angle Finder to determine the angle of the design. Rotate the design on the machine.

Step 3: *Baste the collar to the tulle.*

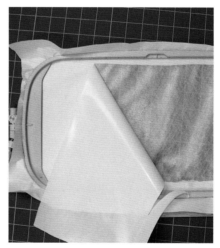

Step 7: *Remove the paper to expose the sticky stabilizer surface.*

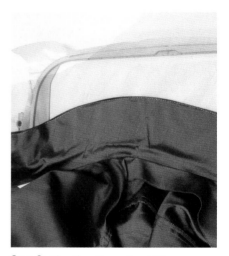

Step 8: *Place the collar on the stabilizer.*

TIP

To determine the position of a mirror-imaged embroidery design, just flip the template over; the design is now mirror-imaged. Of course, you'll have to use the mirror-image key on the machine to duplicate the position.

Embroider the Collar

1. Attach the hoop to the machine.

2. Position the needle over the template's crosshair.

3. Remove the template and place a layer of water-soluble stabilizer over the collar, tulle and sticky stabilizer.

4. Embroider the design.

5. Place template MEF17 on the collar edge, making sure the design connects with the previously stitched design.

6. Position the needle over the template crosshair, remove the template and embroider the design.

7. Continue in this fashion until you are almost at the center back, re-hooping as necessary. After each hooping, trim the excess Aqua Melt and replace it with a new sheet.

8. Position the right collar point of the collar on the stabilizer, making sure the collar corner is in the sewing field.

9. Flip template MEF16 over and place it on the corner, extending a portion of the design off the collar edge.

10. Embroider the design as in steps 1 through 7 until you are almost at the center back.

Step 4: *Embroider the first design.*

TIP

Adding a sheet of water-soluble stabilizer on top of the design area and extending it over the exposed tacky surface of the Aqua Melt protects the embroidery foot from sticking to the hooped, adhesive water-soluble stabilizer.

Step 7: *Embroider the design repeat.*

Step 10: *Embroider the right side of the collar.*

11. Connect the embroidery at the center back by placing template MEF16 over the open area. Overlapping the designs is preferred to leaving any portion of the collar unadorned.

12. Embroider the design.

13. Remove the garment from the hoop.

14. Remove all excess stabilizer by trimming and ultimately washing it away.

15. Place the damp collar on a protected surface (a cookie sheet or Teflon pressing sheet work well).

16. Run the tip of a stencil-cutting tool along the edge of the embroidery to remove the excess tulle. Do this while the embroidery is slightly damp to eliminate the possibility of scorching the embroidery.

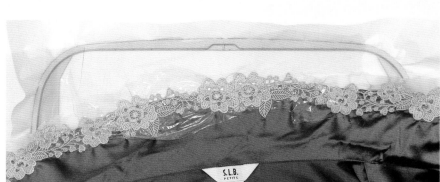

Step 12: *Embroider the design in the center back of the collar.*

Step 16: *Use stencil cutter to remove excess tulle.*

Wear with:

- ∞ fitted silk pants
- ∞ slim pencil skirt
- ∞ believe it or not ... jeans
- ∞ peep-toe shoes and painted toes

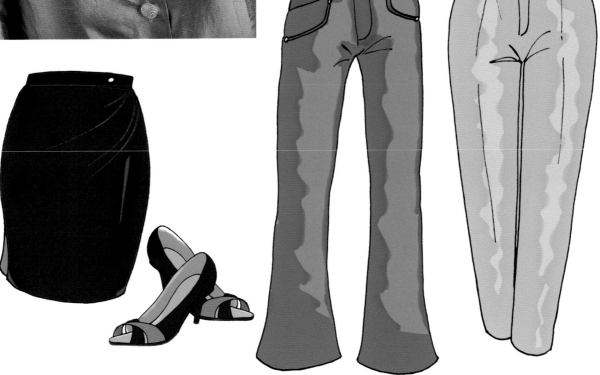

Glam it even more with:

- ∞ a short pearl necklace
- ∞ chandelier earrings
- ∞ a glitzy tennis bracelet

Chapter 5

Princely Pockets

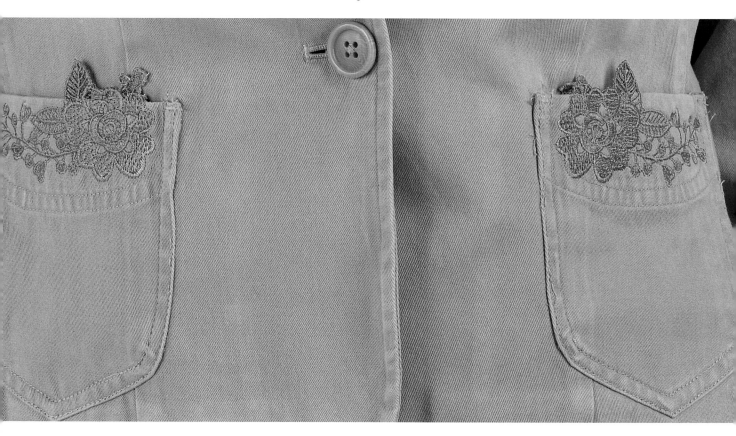

Steps to Success . . .

- Remove excessive decorative stitching on denim pockets if you fear it will detract from the finished monogram.
- Use centering rulers to place single motifs on a pocket.
- If you don't use the back pockets of your jeans for storage, fuse the pocket shut before monogramming. Now you won't have to worry about shifting layers of fabric during the embroidery process.
- Think beyond the pocket! With a little planning, embroidery can be meticulously placed on a pocket and the surrounding area without sacrificing the use of the pocket.
- Consider an asymmetrical design to narrow the silhouette.

Start with the Basics . . .

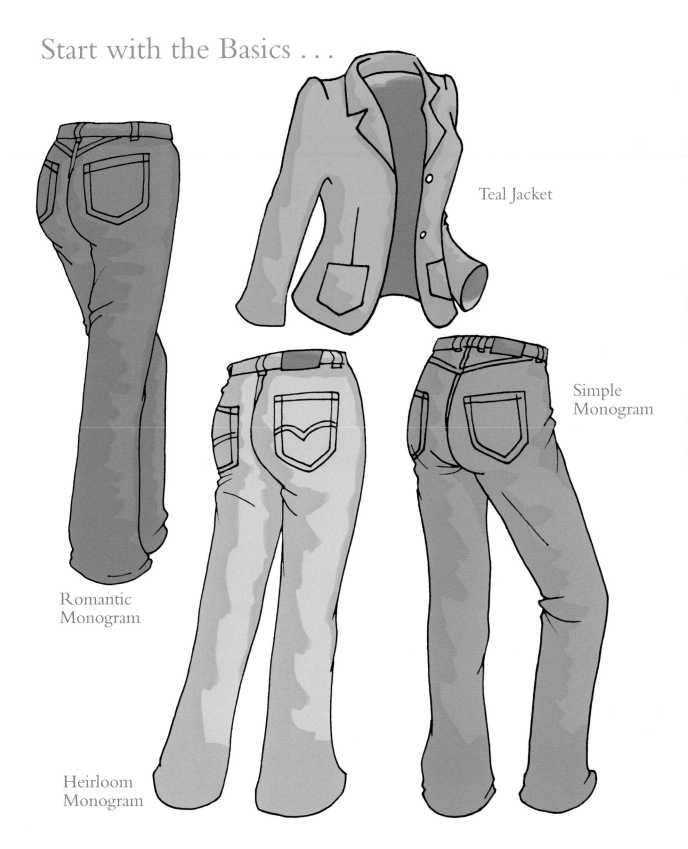

Teal Jacket

Simple
Monogram

Romantic
Monogram

Heirloom
Monogram

Simple Monogram

*The blank
pocket is your
canvas*

Materials

- Blue jeans
- Polymesh stabilizer
- 2 centering rulers
- Paper-backed fusible web
- Target sticker
- Basic machine embroidery and sewing notions
- Lettering software program

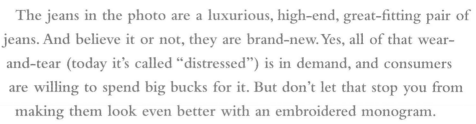

The jeans in the photo are a luxurious, high-end, great-fitting pair of jeans. And believe it or not, they are brand-new. Yes, all of that wear-and-tear (today it's called "distressed") is in demand, and consumers are willing to spend big bucks for it. But don't let that stop you from making them look even better with an embroidered monogram.

I love these jeans. They fit and feel like jeans I've owned for years, yet they are new. When I was a teenager (Oh, here we go!), I lived at the beach, and faded jeans were the only acceptable ensemble at the Saturday night dance. But you couldn't buy faded jeans. The jeans we bought were stiff as cardboard and navy blue—like the pea coats the Coast Guard wore. Yuck!

So resourceful kids that we were, we took our jeans to the bay and drenched them in the salty water against the rocks. And drenched them again and again. It took quite a few drenchings, along with some help from Mom's bottle of bleach in the washing machine, to get that look and feel that we buy off the rack today.

I opted to remove the stitching from this pocket because the original thread was heavy cotton. Due to all of that desirable built-in wear-and-tear, the stitching was also roughed up, leaving tight knots of thread on the surface. I was worried about the monogram's delicate satin stitches covering up the original thread. So I carefully removed the stitching with a seam ripper. It only took a few minutes and was worth the peace of mind.

Prepare the Pocket

1. Slip a 3" square of paper-backed fusible web inside the pocket.

2. Spray the pocket with water and iron the pocket.

3. Let cool and then carefully pull away the protective paper.

4. Smooth the pocket down on the fusible web and iron to fuse the pocket shut.

Step 4: *Prepare pocket with fusible web.*

Plan the Design

1. Find the center of the pocket by placing two centering rulers on the pocket, one vertical and one horizontal. The horizontal ruler is placed at the top of the pocket while the vertical ruler finds the true center of the pocket. Place a target sticker on the zero.

2. Slide the vertical ruler down so the zero is at the bottom of the pocket and measure the pocket in millimeters. Place the zero inside the double welt seam so you are only measuring the design area. This pocket measures 135 mm.

3. Select the font by following the instructions that follow. This font, Fairy Script from Amazing Designs Magnificent Monograms, is a large script letter

Step 1: *Find the pocket's center with centering rulers and then mark it with a target sticker.*

that adds a delicate feminine touch to casual jeans and it was created in a flash.

a. Open a new file in Magnificent Monograms or other lettering program and click on the T icon (text).

b. Select the fabric (denim) and then the font (Fairy Script).

c. Enter just one initial (E) in 80 mm height. An 80 mm height allows for adequate spacing above and below the letter on the pocket and is not so large that the satin stitches will default to a fill stitch in the software.

d. Save the design in the appropriate format and send it to the machine.

Step 2: *Measure the pocket in millimeters.*

Embroider the Pocket

1. Hoop a scrap of denim fabric and cut-away stabilizer.

2. Stitch a sample of the design and analyze it, looking for skipped stitches, bobbin thread appearing on the surface or inadequate thread coverage. If any of these problems occur, take the design back into software and make any needed adjustments.

3. Turn the jeans inside out.

4. Hoop cut-away stabilizer and spray it with temporary adhesive.

5. Center the pocket on the hoop, turning down the waistband so the top edge of the pocket sits just below the edge of the hoop.

Step 5: *Center the pocket in the hoop by turning down the waistband.*

6. Finger-press the pocket to the stabilizer and add pins for extra security.

7. Attach the hoop carefully to the machine and wrap the legs of the jeans around the bed of the machine.

8. Position the needle over the center of the target sticker's crosshair.

9. Remove the target sticker and embroider the design.

10. Remove the hoop from the machine and the jeans from the hoop.

11. Trim the excess stabilizer for the finished look shown.

Step 6: *Press the pocket to the stabilizer, adding pins for extra hold.*

Step 8: *Position the needle over the center of the target sticker.*

Wear with:
- a ruffled white blouse
- brown wedge sandals
- fine jewelry like hoop earrings and a chain necklace

Romantic Monogram

Add a hint of femininity to your favorite pair of pants

Materials

- Corduroy jeans
- Polymesh cutaway stabilizer
- Paper-backed fusible web
- Water-soluble stabilizer
- Tweezers
- Hot-fix applicator
- 25 silver, 4-mm, hot-fix metals
- Temporary spray adhesive
- Target stickers
- Basic machine embroidery and sewing notions
- Single letter monogram (from Embroideryarts Romanesque 2)

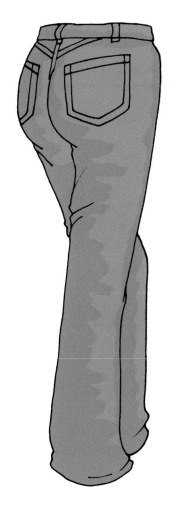

Update a delicate monogram! This feminine single letter monogram gets the star treatment with hot-fix metal nail heads.

Prepare the Pocket

1. Slip a 3" square of paper-backed fusible web inside the pocket.

2. Spray the pocket with water and iron the pocket.

3. Let cool and then carefully pull away the protective paper.

4. Smooth the pocket down on the fusible web and iron to fuse the pocket shut.

Plan the Design

1. Measure to find the center of the pocket, as in step 1 of Plan the Design in the Simple Monogram instructions, page 96, and place a target sticker on the center.

2. Turn the jeans inside out.

Embroider the Pocket

Step 10: *Clear the design area of any trace of water-soluble stabilizer.*

1. Hoop cut-away stabilizer and spray it with temporary adhesive.

2. Center the pocket on the hoop, turning down the top of the pants so the top edge of the pocket sits just below the edge of the hoop.

3. Finger-press the pocket to the stabilizer and add pins for extra security.

4. Attach the hoop carefully to the machine and wrap the legs of the jeans around the bed of the machine.

5. Position the needle over the center of the target sticker's crosshair.

6. Remove the target sticker and lay a piece of water-soluble stabilizer over the design area.

7. Embroider the design.

8. Remove the jeans from the hoop and trim the excess cut-away stabilizer.

9. Tear away the excess water-soluble stabilizer.

10. Take a damp cloth and brush away any remaining bits of water-soluble stabilizer.

TIP

Dawn Weiner, crystal and metal hot-fix expert from www.designbydawn. com, shared this helpful tip with me. She says it's important to protect colored metal nail heads from overexposure to excessive heat from the applicator tools. Cut a small piece of a Teflon protective pressing sheet and place it over the nail head before applying the hot tip. This will keep the nail head from becoming discolored during the fusing process.

Embellish the Embroidery

1. Place the jeans on a flat surface.

2. Use tweezers to place one metal nail head in the center of a flower.

3. Apply the hot, flat tip to the nail head and lift it up.

4. Touch the nail head to the desired location when the glue starts to bubble and hold in position for 20 seconds.

5. Touch the nail head with your finger to make sure it is permanently attached.

6. Repeat steps 2 through 5 on all remaining flower centers for the finished look shown.

Step 2: *Place a metal nail head in a flower center.*

Step 4: *Affix nail head with hot-fix applicator.*

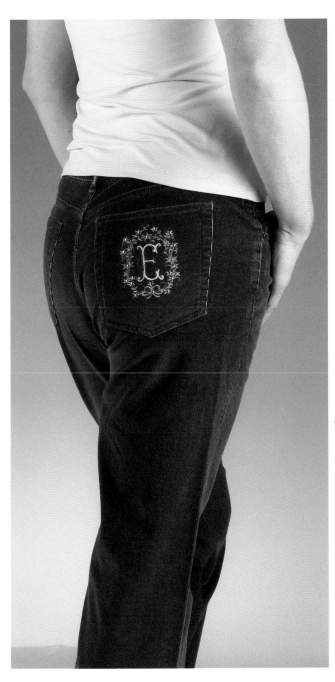

Wear with:

-  a coral sweater
- boots
- a brown belt with silver details

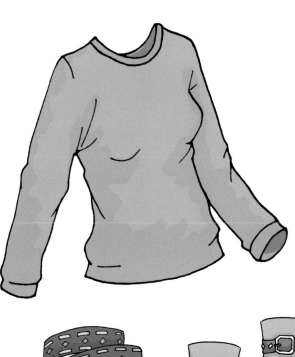

Heirloom Monogram

Silk ribbon adds texture, softness and a special touch of individuality

Materials

- Blue jeans
- Empty bobbin
- 2 yd. 4-mm-wide silk ribbon
- Silk ribbon hand needle
- Self-adhesive tear-away stabilizer
- Water-soluble stabilizer
- Reinforced vinyl
- Masking tape
- Rotary cutter
- Cutting mat
- Monofilament thread
- Temporary spray adhesive
- Basic machine embroidery and sewing notions

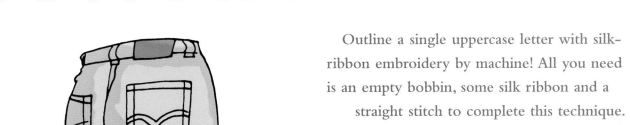

Outline a single uppercase letter with silk-ribbon embroidery by machine! All you need is an empty bobbin, some silk ribbon and a straight stitch to complete this technique. Many jeans already have a decorative stitching detail on the pocket. In fact, it's part of the designer's signature. Look for jeans that have little or no decorative stitching on the pocket. Some jeans, like this pair, may be fine with an embroidered monogram stitched right on top, while others should have all original stitching removed.

Prepare the Pocket

1. Remove one of the back pockets with a seam ripper. Leave the bartack stitches in place at the top of the pocket, as this will make it easier to reattach the pocket.

2. Make a window from reinforced vinyl for the hoop.

3. Cut a piece of vinyl 4" larger than the hoop.

4. Hoop the vinyl and place it on a cutting mat.

5. Use a rotary cutter to cut a window in the vinyl, leaving a 1" frame around the interior of the hoop.

6. Remove the protective paper from the self-adhesive stabilizer and finger-press the sticky surface to the back of the hooped window.

7. Find the center of the pocket with centering rulers and place a target sticker on the center.

8. Lift the pocket away from the jeans and press the pocket to the sticky stabilizer.

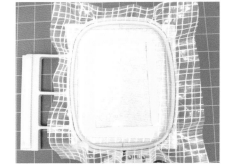

Step 6: *Place the stabilizer on the hooped window.*

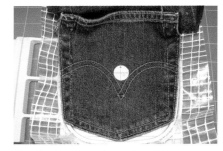

Step 8: *Press the pocket to the stabilizer.*

Embroider the Pocket

1. Attach the hoop to the machine and position the needle over the target sticker.

2. Remove the target sticker.

3. Wrap the jeans carefully around the bed of the machine and embroider the letter.

4. Remove the hoop from the machine and the jeans from the stabilizer.

5. Press the silk ribbon gently to remove any wrinkles.

6. Trim one end of the ribbon on the diagonal to create a long, narrow point.

7. Place an empty bobbin on the bobbin winder and thread the pointed end of the ribbon around the bobbin and through a hole in the top.

8. Set the machine speed at the lowest possible setting and wind the bobbin. Let the ribbon slide through your index finger and thumb as it winds around the bobbin.

9. Place the bobbin in the bobbin case, but do not feed the ribbon through the bobbin case tension.

10. Thread the needle with monofilament thread.

11. Pull up the silk ribbon by turning the handwheel and holding the monofilament thread. Leave a 5" tail.

12. Place the jeans pocket on the sewing bed, wrong side up.

13. Insert the needle right next to the monogram.

14. Select a straight stitch with a 3.0 stitch length.

15. Stitch around the monogram slowly, with the needle penetrating the fabric at the edge of the embroidery. Leave a long thread tail, about 5".

16. Turn the pocket over and inspect the silk ribbon. Small adjustments can be made by gently tugging on the ribbon to distribute the fullness.

17. Use the silk ribbon hand-sewing needle to pull the ribbon tails to the wrong side. Knot the tails on the wrong side and trim.

18. Pin the pocket back into position and sew it in place for the finished look shown.

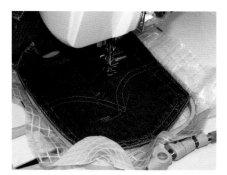

Step 3: *Embroider the letter.*

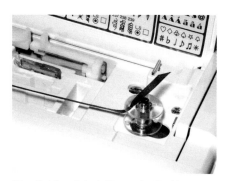

Step 7: *Thread the bobbin with silk ribbon.*

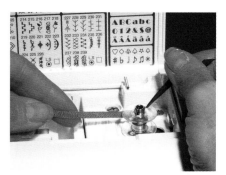

Step 8: *Wind the bobbin, being sure to guide the ribbon as the bobbin spins.*

Step 15: *Stitch around the monogram.*

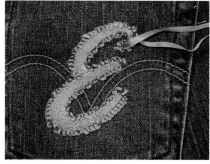

Step 16: *Inspect the silk ribbon, making small adjustments with gentle pulling, if necessary.*

Step 17: *Pull the tails to the wrong side and knot before trimming them off.*

Wear with:

- ❧ royal blue silk blouse with gold buttons
- ❧ flat gold ballet slippers
- ❧ gold clutch

Marigold and cadet blue ...
a timeless color combination.

Teal
Jacket

A touch of lace softens the square pockets

Materials

- Teal cardigan jacket
- dSolv by Hoop It All (water-soluble adhesive stabilizer)
- 2 neutral shade 7" x 5" pieces tulle
- Water-soluble stabilizer
- Seam ripper
- Stencil cutter
- Target sticker
- Basic machine embroidery and sewing notions
- MEF16 embroidery design and template

The most interesting feature of this embroidery treatment is the portion of lace extending off the edge of the pocket. Tulle is used to reinforce the embroidery stitches that extend off the edge. The challenge here is how to hoop!

Prepare the Pocket

1. Place the template on the hemmed edge of the pocket.

2. Slide a target sticker under the template and remove the template.

3. Release the upper portion of the pocket carefully from the jacket with a seam ripper. Leave the stitching intact on the bottom of the pocket. This makes it so easy to reattach the pocket later, just smooth into place and stitch!

4. Fold the jacket away from the pocket and pin the double-fold of the jacket.

5. Peel the protective film off the water-soluble adhesive stabilizer and press the tacky surface to the wrong side of the hoop.

6. Lay the hoop on a cutting mat, lining up one edge of the hoop with a line on the mat.

7. Lay the strip of tulle over the center of the hoop, extending beyond the horizontal sides of the hoop. Insert the inner hoop.

8. Center the pocket on the tulle and stabilizer, lining up the edge of the pocket with a line on the cutting mat.

9. Place one layer of water-soluble stabilizer on top of the pocket and pin all layers.

Step 4: *Fold the pocket away from the jacket and pin the fold.*

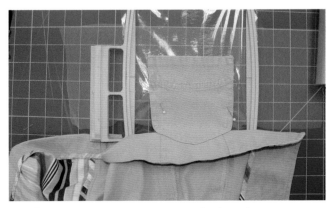

Step 9: *Place water-soluble stabilizer on top of pocket and pin.*

Embroider the Pocket

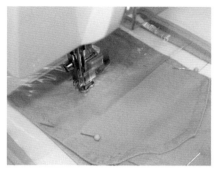

Step 1: *Position the needle over the marked crosshair.*

1. Place the hoop on the machine and position the needle over the marked crosshair.

2. Wrap the jacket carefully around the bed of the machine. If necessary, reposition the embroidery machine on the table to accommodate the jacket bulk. It's imperative the weight of the jacket is supported and not left hanging over the edge of the table.

3. Embroider the design.

4. Remove the hoop from the machine, unpin the pocket and remove it from the hoop.

5. Tear off the water-soluble stabilizer.

6. Use a stencil cutter to trim the tulle.

7. Sew the pocket back in place.

8. Repeat all steps on the other pocket for the finished look shown.

Step 6: *Trim the tulle with a stencil cutter.*

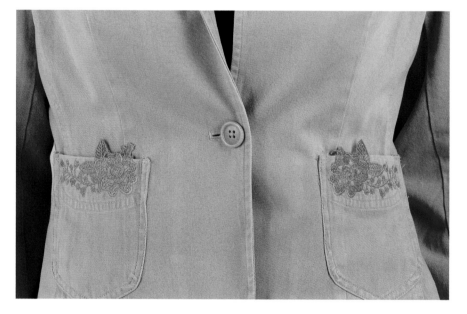

Wear with:
- khakis
- brown slacks
- a lace skirt
- a lace-trimmed cami

Chapter 6 Exotic Edges

Steps to Success . . .

- Examine the edge carefully. Is it hemmed, faced or serged? Embroidering on hemmed edges may be easier if the hem is released before embroidering and sewn after all embellishment. Faced edges can be stitched through both layers, or the facing can be temporarily removed.

- Since you're embroidering on the edge of a garment, always place the bulk of the garment away from the arm/head of the machine. Let the garment rest around the machine instead of being balled up under the machine.

- Turn the garment inside-out so only a single layer of fabric is hooped. "Open" the garment to expose the design area. Pin or clip the rest of the garment out of harm's way.

Start with the Basics . . .

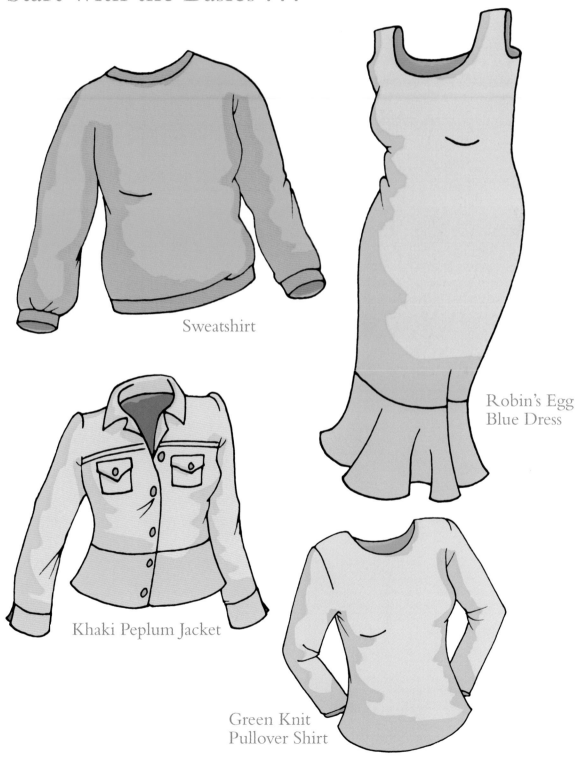

Sweatshirt

Robin's Egg
Blue Dress

Khaki Peplum Jacket

Green Knit
Pullover Shirt

Robin's Egg Blue Dress with Bias Ruffle

This linen sheath with bias ruffle is perfect for a garden party

Materials

- Linen sheath with bias ruffle
- Tear-away stabilizer
- Metafil needle size 80
- Temporary spray adhesive
- Target stickers
- Basic machine embroidery and sewing notions
- MEF7 embroidery design and template

A sprinkle of polka dots adds a tiny splash of color to the kicky ruffle on this sheath. I used four bright shades of rayon embroidery thread and stitched a feminine floral ribbon trim to the neck and the seamline where the ruffle meets the dress.

Plan the Design

1. Press the ruffle.

2. Place the dress on a flat surface and smooth the ruffle.

3. Place target stickers in a grid pattern on the ruffle, starting at the center front. Since the target stickers are larger than the small polka dots, place the stickers closer together than appears necessary. On the sample, the stitches are 4" apart. Label each sticker with an initial to represent the thread color. I used "Y" for yellow, "P" for pink, "G" for green and "PP" for purple. Try to scatter the thread colors sporadically.

4. Turn the dress inside out.

Step 3: *Scatter target stickers throughout the design area on the ruffle.*

Embroider the Ruffle

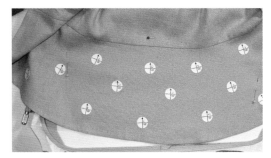

Step 3: *Pin the ruffle to the stabilizer.*

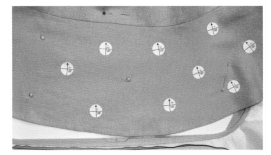

Step 7: *Embroider all the pink dots first.*

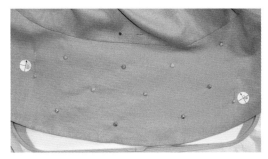

Step 9: *Finish stitching the dots.*

Step 16: *Prepare the side areas for stitching.*

1. Hoop tear-away stabilizer in the largest hoop available and spray it with temporary adhesive.

2. Finger-press the ruffle onto the sticky stabilizer, smoothing out the ruffle.

3. Pin the ruffle to the stabilizer away from the target stickers for extra security.

4. Thread the machine with the first color, pink.

5. Attach the hoop to the machine and position the needle over the cross-hair of a P-labeled target sticker.

6. Remove the target sticker and embroider the small dot (MEF7).

7. Move to the next P target sticker and repeat the process until all of the pink dots have been embroidered.

8. Thread the needle with the next color, green, and embroider all of the green dots.

9. Repeat for yellow and purple.

10. Remove the hoop from the machine.

11. Remove the dress and stabilizer from the hoop.

12. Trim all threads from the right and wrong side of the embroidery.

13. Carefully tear away the excess stabilizer from the wrong side of the ruffle.

14. Use the first embroidered section as a guide to place target stickers on the center back.

15. Repeat the steps above to embroider the center back of the ruffle.

16. Connect the center front and back embroidered sections. Use the target stickers to repeat the spacing as before. If the same spacing will not fit, omit a row or two at the side seams.

17. Repeat all steps until the entire ruffle is embroidered for the finished look shown.

Wear with:
- ❧ strappy sandals
- ❧ a stylish purse
- ❧ a spring in your step

Green
Knit
Pullover
Shirt

Delicious shades of sherbet ... so refreshing

Materials

- Knit pullover
- Fusible polymesh stabilizer
- Paisley embroidery designs
- Target stickers
- Basic machine embroidery and sewing notions
- MEF7 and MEF21 embroidery designs and templates

Jazz up a simple pullover shirt with elegant embroidery at the hem. Two embroidery designs are evenly spaced in a horizontal line to create the hem border on the green polo. A corner design is added to define the space. It's easy to do this in embroidery customizing software.

TIP

To test a design for knit fabric, add water-soluble stabilizer on top of the design area and embroider the designs on a fabric scrap. Scrutinize the embroidery, looking closely at the outline stitches. Has the registration on the design shifted? That can indicate two things: not enough stabilizer or a damaged needle. Turn the hoop over and look at the wrong side of the embroidery. Is the tension correct? The bobbin thread should be one-third of all the thread on the wrong side.

Now remove the fabric from the hoop and carefully tear away the excess water-soluble stabilizer. Does the fabric bubble up around the embroidery or does the fabric lay flat? Bubbling is a sign of embroidery designs that are too dense. Often, the embroidery looks perfect until the fabric is released from the hoop, then the fabric relaxes and bubbles. "Designs in Machine Embroidery" Ask the Expert columnist, Deborah Jones, showed me this handy test for density. Roll the fabric into a tube and notice how the embroidered area rolls. If it flattens in a stiff manner, the stitch count is too high for the fabric.

Roll the fabric in a tube to test how the embroidered area rolls. If it's stiff, the stitch count is too high.

Plan the Design

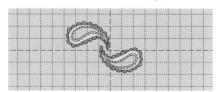

Figure 6-1

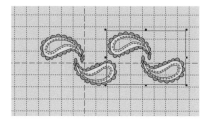

Figure 6-2

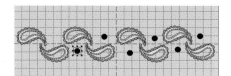

Step 13: *Place dots from right to left.*

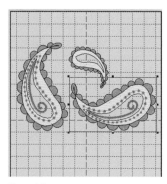

Step 16: *Arrange the corner design.*

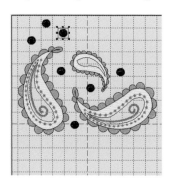

Step 17: *Fill the open areas with dots.*

1. Open a new file in customizing software and select a large hoop.

2. Copy design MEF21 into the file.

3. Travel through the design and remove colors 1 and 6. Resize the design to 45 mm x 32 mm. Save it as MEF21small.

4. Copy the design again and mirror-image it, vertically and horizontally.

5. Move the design so it creates a horizontal line (Figure 6-1).

6. Select both designs (CTRL A) and copy and paste.

7. Move the paisley designs to the right of the first set (Figure 6-2).

8. Repeat this process until the hoop is filled.

9. Save the design as Paisley Border.

10. Open design MEF7 and copy and paste it into Paisley Border.

11. Fill each open area with a dot.

12. Copy and paste in an organized manner. Insert the first dot next to the last paisley design placed. If the last paisley is on the far right, place the first dot there.

13. Continue placing the dots from the right to the left.

14. Remove the color stops between each dot so the dots stitch as one color.

15. Save the design, print a template of it and send it to the embroidery machine.

16. Open design MEF21 and copy it (twice) into a new file to create the corner design. Copy MEF21small into the file. Arrange the three designs as shown.

17. Copy and paste design MEF7 into the file. Fill the open areas with a dot.

18. Save the design as Corner Paisley, print a template of it and send it to the machine.

19. Center the Paisley Border template 2" above the hem on the shirt.

20. Slide a target sticker under the template aligning the crosshairs and remove the template.

21. Turn the shirt inside out and iron the fusible polymesh stabilizer to the wrong side of the polo shirt, extending the stabilizer 3" below the hem.

TIP

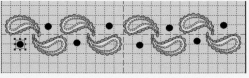

When manipulating designs in customizing software, it makes sense to plan your steps. Start at one end of the design and continue across the sewing field. Work in a logical path to cut down on the travel time between stitches and to keep the registration of the design in place during the stitching process.

Embroider the Shirt

1. Hoop the stabilizer and shirt, centering the target sticker in the hoop. Pin the shirt to the stabilizer for added stability.

2. Attach the hoop to the machine and position the needle over the target sticker.

3. Remove the target sticker and place a piece of water-soluble stabilizer over the design area.

4. Embroider the design.

5. Remove the fabric from the hoop.

6. Trim the excess polymesh stabilizer.

7. Lay the shirt on a flat surface, place a ruler under the embroidered border and chalk a straight line from the end of the embroidery to the side seam.

8. Place the Corner Paisley Template on the shirt so the bottom edge of the Corner Paisley sits on the chalked line.

9. Slide a target sticker under the template, aligning the crosshairs, and remove the template.

10. Iron a new piece of fusible polymesh stabilizer to fit a smaller hoop (5" x 7") to the wrong side of the shirt.

11. Center the Corner Paisley target sticker in a vertical fashion and hoop the shirt.

12. Add water-soluble stabilizer on top of the design area and embroider the Corner design.

13. Repeat steps 5 through 12 on the opposite corner for the finished look shown.

Step 4: *Embroider the shirt.*

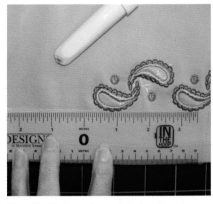

Step 7: *Chalk-mark a straight line from the embroidery to the side seam.*

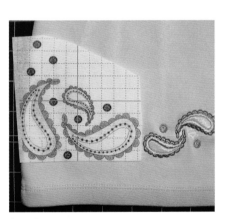

Step 8: *Place the template on the shirt, using the chalk line as a guide.*

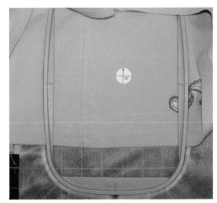

Step 12: *Add water-soluble stabilizer to the top of the shirt before stitching the corner.*

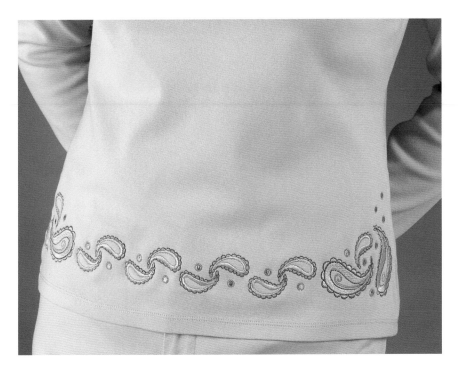

Wear with:
- khakis
- a white eyelet skirt
- canvas slides
- a traditional tote with rope sandals

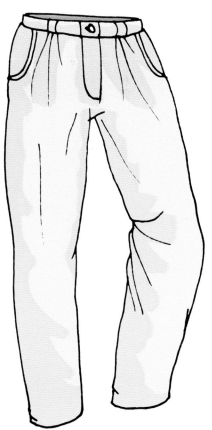

Khaki Peplum Jacket

Add instant impact with free-form appliqués and transform ultrasuede swatches into an exotic edge treatment

Materials

- Jacket with peplum
- Sensuede: light blue, slate blue, medium brown, beige, light green and avocado
- Polymesh stabilizer
- Stencil cutter
- Teflon pressing sheet or cookie sheet
- Angle finder
- Temporary spray adhesive
- Target stickers
- Basic machine embroidery and sewing notions
- MEF1, MEF10 and MEF26 embroidery designs and templates

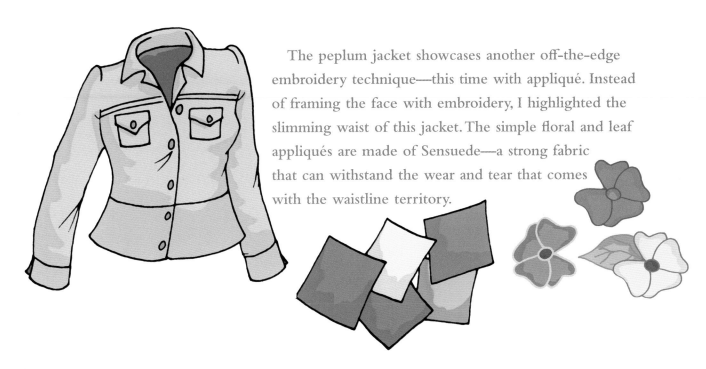

The peplum jacket showcases another off-the-edge embroidery technique—this time with appliqué. Instead of framing the face with embroidery, I highlighted the slimming waist of this jacket. The simple floral and leaf appliqués are made of Sensuede—a strong fabric that can withstand the wear and tear that comes with the waistline territory.

Plan the Design

1. Try the jacket on and audition the templates on the jacket.

2. Scatter some of the designs off the edge of the jacket. Look for flattering placement. If you have a tiny waist, place the designs up near the waist in the jacket. Color helps also; keep the light colors in the center of the figure and the darker shades toward the side seams of the jacket. Overlap the templates for a lush and luxurious appliqué display.

3. Take the jacket off and place it on a flat work surface.

4. Slide target stickers under the templates, aligning the crosshairs.

5. Write the design numbers on the target stickers. Pay special attention to the overlapped designs and determine the sequence of the overlapped designs. Mark the design that will be partially obstructed by another design as #1. Number each one accordingly.

6. Remove the templates carefully.

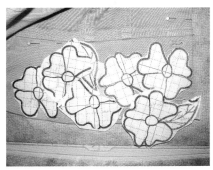

Step 3: *Place the jacket on a flat work surface so you can see the templates easily.*

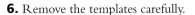

TIP

When layering appliqué designs, take the translucence of the fabric into consideration. Dense fabrics such as Sensuede will not bleed through each other. However, lighter fabrics may appear as a shadow under an appliqué design. At times, this can be desirable, but careful analysis should take place during the testing phase.

Embroider the Jacket

1. Hoop polymesh stabilizer in a large hoop, if available.

2. Spray the wrong side of the left jacket with temporary adhesive and finger-press the jacket onto the sticky stabilizer.

3. Pin the jacket, making sure the pins are out of the sewing field.

4. Select the first design and position the needle over the first target sticker.

Step 6: *Stitch the first color.*

5. Use the Angle Finder to determine the rotation of the design if necessary. Rotate the design on the machine screen.

6. Remove the target sticker and stitch the first color, the placement guide.

7. Place a piece of appliqué fabric over the placement guide, making sure the appliqué fabric covers the placement guide.

8. Stitch the second color, the tack down.

9. Carefully remove the hoop from the machine, but <u>do not remove the stabilizer or garment from the hoop.</u>

10. Trim away the excess fabric as close as possible to the tack-down stitching.

11. Return the hoop to the machine and complete the design.

12. Move the needle to the next target sticker and repeat the process.

13. Remove the garment from the hoop once all the appliqués are embroidered on the left peplum.

14. Repeat the process for the right peplum.

15. Mirror-image the designs for a balanced look. Pay special attention to the colors of the appliqués. Try to evenly spread the colors across both the right and left peplums. Look at the whole jacket, not just one side when deciding where to place each color.

16. Slide a protective surface (such as a cookie sheet or Teflon pressing sheet) under the peplum after all embroidery is complete.

17. Heat a stencil cutter and use it to remove the excess stabilizer extending below the peplum.

18. Run the hot tip close to the embroidery threads and the nylon polymesh will melt and shrink into the embroidery for the finished look shown.

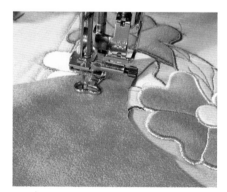

Step 7: *Place the appliqué fabric over the stitched placement guide.*

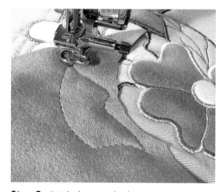

Step 8: *Stitch the second color.*

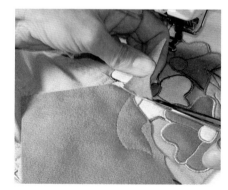

Step 10: *Trim the excess appliqué fabric.*

Alternative Appliqué Method

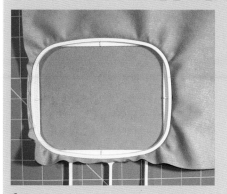

1. Select a hoop that will accommodate as many designs as possible. Hoop the appliqué fabric without stabilizer. Load as many repeats of one design that the hoop will hold. Stitch only the first color, the placement guide, of each design.

2. Remove the fabric from the hoop and cut the appliqués on the placement line. Be careful to trim exactly on the line.

3. Hoop the jacket as instructed in steps 2 and 3 of the main instructions, and stitch the first color of the design.

4. Spray the wrong side of the appliqué with temporary adhesive and position it on the placement line. Finger-press the appliqué to the garment.

5. Stitch the second color, the tack down, and then finish the design.

TIP

Appliqués that extend off the edge of the jacket need a little more attention during the stitching process. Since the embroidery foot will travel beyond the edge of the appliqué, there's a pretty good chance the foot will slide under the appliqué.

This can create quite a mess, so stay with the machine and keep a close eye on the foot during the tack-down segment. Use tweezers or a bamboo skewer to hold down the appliqué. Also, firmly pressing the sticky side (the wrong side) of the appliqué onto the polymesh stabilizer helps flatten the edge of the appliqué and reduces the chance of catching the foot underneath the appliqué.

Wear with:
- jeans
- flat-front skirt
- suede shoes and bag

Sweatshirt

*The plain
sweatshirt . . .
it's time for a
makover*

Materials

- Sweatshirt
- Polymesh stabilizer
- Water-soluble stabilizer
- Chalko Liner
- Quilter's ruler
- Centering rulers
- Tracing paper
- ½ yd. cotton quilting fabric (bias binding)
- Monofilament thread
- Temporary spray adhesive
- Basic machine embroidery and sewing notions
- MEF12 embroidery design and template

America has an ongoing love affair with sweatshirts. It started in our youth, when we wore them for warmth. And then in our teens and 20s, it became fashionable to wear our sweetheart's sweatshirt—oversized and well-worn. Later, we slid into one every weekend because it didn't matter what we wore to clean house—it was comfort clothing. Then we loved sweatshirts because they wash and wear so well and blend right in with the rest of the family's laundry. But sweatshirts don't have to be sloppy, drab and oversized. They can be fashionable, colorful and fitted. Start with a favorite colored sweatshirt, snip here and there, march some flowers down the front, and finish it with a contrasting binding. Sweatshirts never looked this good!

Prepare the Sweatshirt

1. Cut away the ribbing at the hem and sleeves.

2. Fold the sweatshirt in half, shoulder seam to shoulder seam, to find the true center front. Mark the center at the neckline.

3. Lay the sweatshirt on a flat surface. Place a quilter's ruler on the center front, using the mark and the shirt's lower edge as a guide. Chalk a vertical line from neck to hem on the center front.

4. Cut the sweatshirt open at the side seams, from the waist to the sleeve.

Cut ...
≈ off the ribbing
≈ open the side seams

Stitch ...
≈ beautiful symmetrical embroidery
≈ a bias binding

Plan the Design

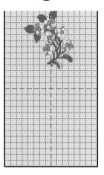

Figure 6-3

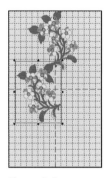

Figure 6-4

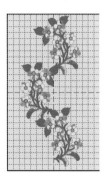

Figure 6-5

1. Open a new file in customizing software.

2. Select the largest hoop for your machine.

3. Copy and paste design MEF12 into the hoop. Move it to the top of the hoop and rotate it slightly (Figure 6-3).

4. Copy and paste another repeat of MEF12.

5. Move the second repeat below the first one.

6. Mirror-image the design and connect it to the first one (Figure 6-4).

7. Select and copy the repeat of MEF12 that's positioned at the top of the hoop.

8. Paste it below the second repeat to create a continuous line of embroidery (Figure 6-5). Focus on the outer edges of the three designs. Make sure the designs fill the same amount of space horizontally.

9. Save the design as Sweatshirt Border in the appropriate format.

10. Print four templates of Sweatshirt Border.

11. Place the Sweatshirt Border templates on the sweatshirt, equidistant from the center front, creating two parallel, vertical borders.

12. Slide target stickers under the templates and remove the templates.

TIP

Although there are 24 color changes in Sweatshirt Border, I did not color sort the design since the three repeats of MEF12 (which make up Sweatshirt Border) overlap each other. When the color sort feature is used on overlapped designs, the results are not always desirable. If your software program has the ability to eliminate stitches that lay under overlapped areas, use it and then color sort the design. Otherwise, do what I often do, change the thread 24 times! It gives very predictable results, which is a good thing in a fast-paced life.

Embroider the Sweatshirt

1. Hoop polymesh stabilizer and spray it with temporary adhesive.

2. Position the upper portion of the sweatshirt front in the hoop.

3. Finger-press the sweatshirt to the sticky stabilizer and pin it for extra security.

4. Attach the hoop to the machine and position the needle over the first target sticker.

5. Remove the target sticker and add a layer of water-soluble stabilizer on top of the design area.

6. Embroider the design.

7. Position the needle over the target sticker opposite the first design.

8. Remove the target sticker and add a layer of water-soluble stabilizer on top of the design area. Embroider the design.

9. Remove the hoop from the machine and the sweatshirt from the hoop.

10. Hoop a new piece of stabilizer and spray it with temporary adhesive.

11. Position the lower part of the sweatshirt in the hoop.

12. Attach the hoop to the machine and position the needle over the target sticker.

13. Remove the target sticker and add a layer of water-soluble stabilizer on top of the design area.

14. Embroider the design and repeat for the remaining design.

15. Remove the hoop from the machine and the sweatshirt from the hoop.

16. Trim the stabilizer from the wrong side of the garment and tear off the excess water-soluble stabilizer.

Finish the Sweatshirt

1. Chalk a curving line around the perimeter of the embroidery at the center front on the right front.

2. Cut the sweatshirt on the straight center front line.

3. Staystitch on the chalked curving line on the right front.

4. Trim the excess fabric, leaving ½" seam allowance.

5. Use the scrap fabric as a guide for trimming the left front.

6. Place the scrap on the left front, right side down, matching the straight side of the scrap with the straight edge of the left front.

7. Trim around the scrap.

8. Cut the ribbing off the neck.

9. Staystitch the left front and neck ½" from the edge.

10. Cut 2¾" bias strips. Seam the strips together to create one long 3-yd. length.

11. Press the strip in half lengthwise.

12. Place the strip on the right side of the sweatshirt, matching raw edges.

13. Sew with a ½" seam allowance overlapping the ends.

Step 8: *Cut the ribbing from the neck.*

Step 15: *Detail of finished embroidered edge.*

14. Press the bias binding to the wrong side of the sweatshirt.

15. Stitch in the ditch on the front to catch the seam allowance on the wrong side. Use monofilament thread to hide the stitches.

Oops!

When I started embroidering the second Sweatshirt Border, I noticed that the designs were not equidistant from the center front. Yikes! It was off nearly an inch! To correct this mistake, I placed a centering ruler on the sweatshirt with the zero on the center front. Then I placed the template the same distance from the center front as the first embroidered design, concentrating on the small leaf at the top of the design. Then I slid a new target sticker into the correct location and positioned the needle over it. I didn't bother removing the stitches at this time. I pulled them out after all the embroidery was complete because I knew some would be hidden behind the leaves. I'm not one for initiating any unnecessary ripping!

Wear with:
- jeans
- a colorful tank
- tennis shoes
- carry-on tote

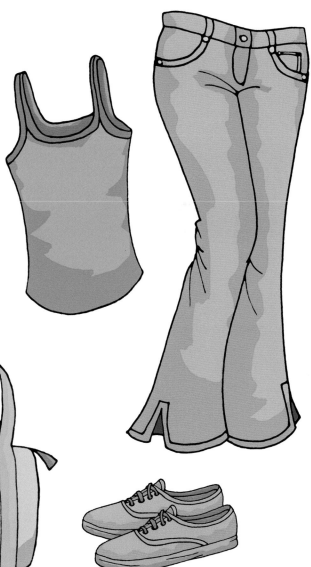

Resources

Products

Designs in Machine Embroidery
In The Hoop Tool Kit, Perfect
Placement Kit, Perfect Towel Kit
(888) 739-0555
www.dzgns.com

Embroidery Designs

Adorable Ideas Designs
(866) 492-3337
www.adorableideas.com

Amazing Designs
(866) 336-8329
www.amazingdesigns.com

Bobbi Bullard
(530) 333-1964
www.bullarddesigns.com

Cactus Punch
(800) 487-6972
www.cactuspunch.com

Creative Design
www.creativedesign.com

Criswell Embroidery & Design
www.k-lace.com

Designs in Machine Embroidery
(888) 739-0555
www.dzgns.com

Embroideryarts
(888) 238-1372
www.embroideryarts.com

Embroidery Central
(800) 428-7606
www.embroidery.com

Holley Berry Collections
www.holleyberry.com

Laura's Sewing Studio
(866) 844-8895
www.laurassewingstudio.com

Martha Pullen
(800) 547-4176 ext. 2
www.marthapullen.com

OESD
(405) 359-2741
www.embroideryonline.com

**Smart Needle Embroidery
Collection**
(248) 807-8726
www.smartneedle.com

**Stitchitize Embroidery Design
Service**
(800) 667-2587
www.stitchitize.com

Vermillion Stitchery
(940) 725-0163
www.vsccs.com

Crystals, Beads and Embellishments

Design by Dawn
(910) 397-9061
www.designbydawn.com

Sue's Sparklers
(760) 745-2510
www.suessparklers.com

Embroidery Machines

Baby Lock
(800) 422-2952
www.babylock.com

Bernina
(800) 405-2739
www.berninausa.com

Brother International Corp.
(800) 422-7684
www.brothersews.com

Husqvarna/Viking
(800) 358-0001
www.husqvarnaviking.com

Janome
(800) 631-0183
www.janome.com

Pfaff
(800) 997-3233
www.pfaff.com

Singer
(800) 474-6437
www.singershop.com

Software

**Amazing Designs Magazine (see
Embroidery Designs listing)**

**Brother (see Embroidery Machines
listing)**

**Bernina (see Embroidery Machines
listing)**

**Baby Lock (see Embroidery
Machines listing)**

Buzz Tools
www.buzztools.com

Generations
(636) 724-5800
www.generationsemb.com

**Husqvarna/Viking (see
Embroidery Machines listing)**

**OESD (see Embroidery Designs
listing)**

Origins
(866) 678-7638
www.originssoftware.com

Pfaff (see Embroidery Machines listing)

Singer (see Embroidery Machines listing)

Thread

Coats & Clark
(800) 648-1479
www.coatsandclark.com

Madeira
(603) 528-2944
www.madeirausa.com

Mettler
(800) 847-3235
www.amefird.com/mettler.htm

Robison-Anton Textile Company
(201) 941-0500
www.robison-anton.com

Sulky of America
(800) 874-4115
www.sulky.com

Stabilizers

Floriani Sewing & Quilting Products
(877) 331-0034
www.rnkdistributing.com

Hoop-It-All
(800) 847-4911
www.hoopitall.com

HTCW Products
(800) 275-4275
www.htcwproducts.net

Madeira (see Thread listing)

OESD (see Embroidery Designs listing)

Sulky of America (see Thread listing)

Husqvarna/Viking (see Embroidery Machines listing)

Supplies

Ann The Gran
www.annthegran.com

Nancy's Notions
(800) 833-0690
www.nancynotions.com

Shoppers Rule
www.shoppersrule.com

Magazines

Creative Machine Embroidery
(800) 677-5212
www.cmemag.com

Designs in Machine Embroidery
Edited by Eileen Roche
(888) 739-0555
www.dzgns.com

Sew Beautiful
(800) 547-4176
www.marthapullen.com

Sewing Savvy
(800) 449-0440
www.clotildesewingsavvy.com

Sew News
(800) 289-6397
www.sewnews.com

Threads
(800) 888-8286
www.ThreadsMagazine.com

Books

Krause Publications
(800) 258-0929
www.krause.com

Acknowledgments

Writing this book was fun—not sheer joy—but definitely fun!

It was a pleasure to shop, search for the right blanks, draw the embroidery designs, test the embroidery designs, design the embroidery layouts for each project and then finally stitch the projects. And that was just the first two months.

Then I moved on to writing, editing and photography. And published four issues of *Designs in Machine Embroidery* during the process.

People often asked, "How did you do it?"

Well, I was inspired by my parents. In January, 2005, my father, Pat Ward, was diagnosed with life-threatening bone cancer. Faced with two gruesome choices, he chose the most difficult path. He chose to fight the cancer and had his jaw replaced at the ripe age of 76. His daily struggle with nutrition, strength and hope was difficult to witness. And unfortunately, I didn't witness it daily, as he lives 1,400 miles away. It was painful to hear of his struggles through my sisters and mom. And later, my dad was able to tell me himself.

But he never complained. He always focused on the great care that my mom and sisters gave him. He thought the secret to his improving health was through their loving acts. He wondered, out loud, how cancer patients fought the fight without the aid of family.

My mother, Betty, made it her daily mission to take charge of his nutrition. She wanted him to thrive—to get back to living, to get back to storytelling, to get back to his old self. And he has—almost. There have been trade-offs, but we are so thankful for this gift of time, another year with him.

So when I thought I was too tired to work on the book at night or on the weekends, I just thought of my dad, mom and sisters. I thought how each minute of the fight made him stronger, how my mother never missed a feeding or medication, how my sisters, Mary Pat Palombo and Liz Scully, restructured their lives to help him. How my brother-in-law, Aldo Palombo, watched his wife devote so much of her time to her parents, how he stepped in and provided every possible comfort to his in-laws, including time and companionship.

And so I just plowed on and counted my blessings that my struggle was only with my editor, Maria Turner, and the impending deadlines. Maria kept me on target and was a delight to work with and then right before she left for a new chapter in her life, she gave me one more blessing. She brought me Deborah Peyton, whose wonderful illustrations breathed life and hope into these pages.

I've been blessed in so many ways ....

About the Author

Considered an expert in the machine embroidery field, Eileen is founder and editor of *Designs in Machine Embroidery* magazine and author of *Contemporary Machine-Embroidered Quilts* (Krause Publications, 2004). She began the magazine in 1994 as a newsletter and has grown it into the industry's leading source of inspiration for the home embroidery enthusiast. A love of fabric, thread and texture led Eileen to embroidery, where she was able to combine all three. And a love of fashion brought her to the idea for this book.

Designs in Machine Embroidery is a project-based magazine published six times a year. Editorial content includes machine-embroidered fashions, quilts, home décor and crafts. Check out the newest feature: *Designs Plus!*—a free email newsletter sent monthly to your inbox. Each newsletter features a project, embroidery tips, and the newest products in the market. For more information, please visit www.dzgns.com.

CD-ROM Embroidery Designs (For color sequences, see CD.)

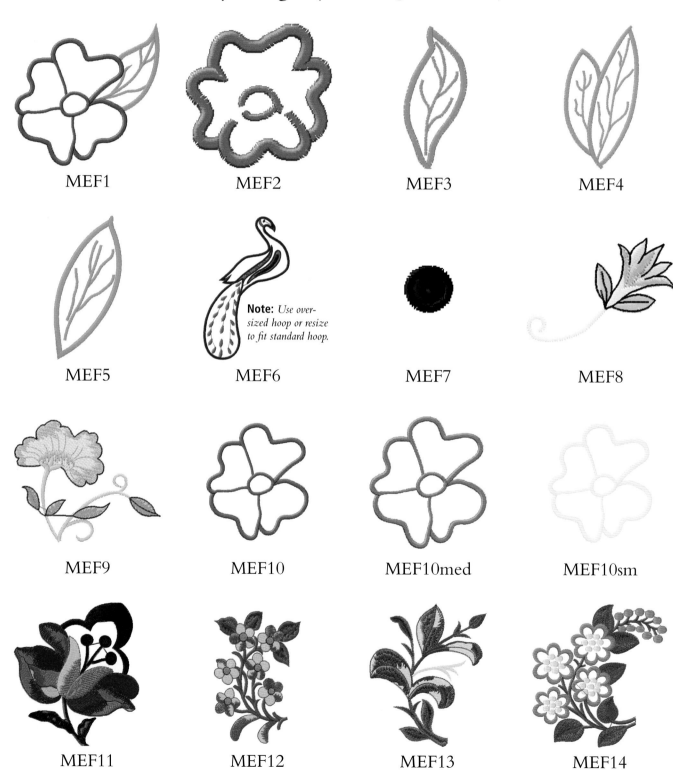

MEF1

MEF2

MEF3

MEF4

MEF5

MEF6

Note: *Use oversized hoop or resize to fit standard hoop.*

MEF7

MEF8

MEF9

MEF10

MEF10med

MEF10sm

MEF11

MEF12

MEF13

MEF14

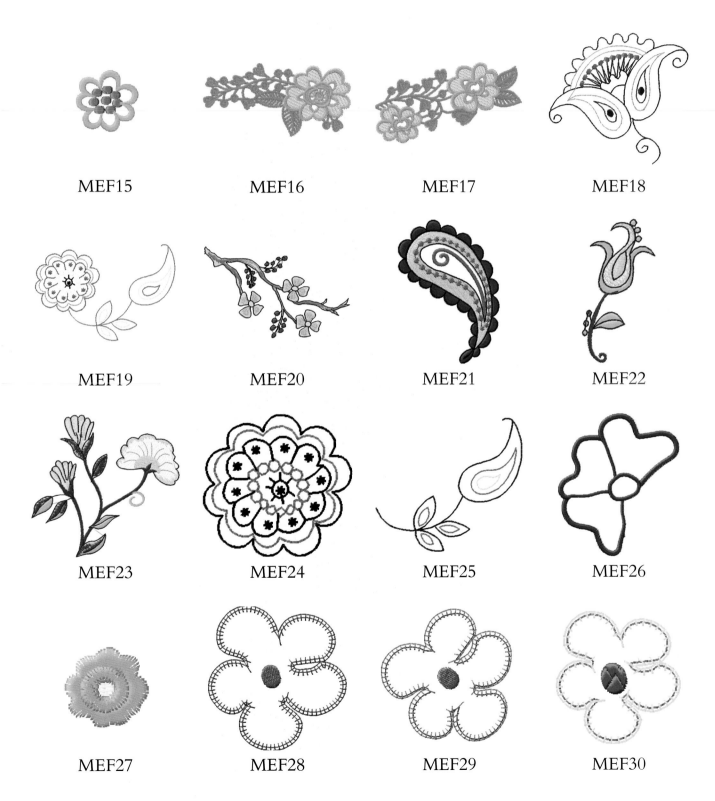

MEF15   MEF16   MEF17   MEF18

MEF19   MEF20   MEF21   MEF22

MEF23   MEF24   MEF25   MEF26

MEF27   MEF28   MEF29   MEF30

INDEX

Angle Finder, 24, 28, 34, 36, 38, 70, 72, 80, 88, 122, 124

Beads, 11, 38, 134

Beaded Tape, 38

Blank, 3, 8, 11, 13, 94

Blouse, 31-35, 61, 70-73, 75, 86-87, 89, 91, 97, 105

Boho, 48, 73

Brown, 12, 52, 55, 61, 66-67, 69, 97, 101, 109, 122

Button, 11, 28-29, 49, 51, 53, 68

Cardigan, 12, 31, 40-43, 63, 106

Centering Rulers, 25, 48, 92, 94, 96, 103, 128

Color Sorting, 16

Crosshair, 18, 23-25, 28, 34, 53-54, 84, 89, 97, 100, 108, 114

Cuff, 18, 48-49, 51, 74, 83-84

Dress, 36-39, 111-115

Editing, 14-15, 26-27, 136

Embroidery Designs

       Manipulating, 118

       Mirror Image, 16, 33

       Organizing, 17

       Sizing, 14-15

       Styles, 29

Embroidery Layout, 11-12

Embroidery Machines, 18, 26, 134-135

Flower, 14, 56, 58, 63-64, 100

Green, 40, 111, 113-114, 116-117, 119, 121-122

Hem, 3, 8, 38, 45-47, 63, 74, 77-78, 84, 110, 117-118, 129

Hooping, 18, 20, 23-24, 29, 50, 64, 89

Hoop Tension, 23, 28

Khaki, 111, 122-123, 125, 127

Monochromatic, 29, 35, 63

Monograms, 96, 105

Off-The-Edge Technique, 87, 107, 108

Paisley, 83, 116, 118

Pants, 8-9, 12, 35, 43, 47, 75, 82-83, 85, 91, 98, 100

Pullover, 11, 61-63, 65, 111, 116-117, 119, 121

Red, 24, 61-63, 65, 72

Removing Pockets, 8, 34, 64, 132

Ribbon, 11, 30, 32-34, 36, 38, 102-104, 113

Satin Stitch, 34

Sequencing, 16, 52

Sheath, 11, 31, 36-39, 71, 112-113

Silk, 75, 86-87, 89, 91, 102-105

Sketch, 11-13

Skirt, 9, 43, 55, 65, 69, 71, 91, 109, 121, 127

Stabilizers

       Cut-away, 20-21, 29, 60, 96, 100

       Tear-away, 20-21, 34, 60, 76, 102, 112, 114

       Wash-away, 21, 60

Sweatshirt, 5, 111, 128-133

Tape, 13, 19, 23, 33, 36, 38-39, 48, 50, 57, 77, 79, 83, 88, 102

Target Stickers, 18, 24-25

Teal, 93, 106-107, 109

Templates, 13, 18-19

Tension, 8, 20, 23, 28-29, 104, 117

Thigh, 45-46

Tools, 13-14, 24, 100, 134, 143

Tricot knit interfacing, 40-41, 62-63

Tweed, 31, 56-59

If you love your copy of "Contemporary Machine-Embroidered Fashions," then you'll definitely want these other fabulous machine embroidery books as well!

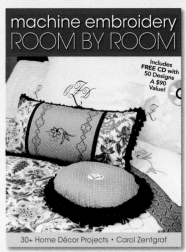

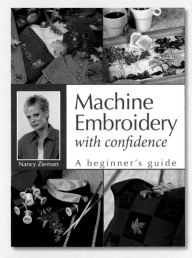

Contemporary Machine Embroidered Quilts
Innovative Techniques and Designs
by Eileen Roche

Moves from the basics of material selection and design, to twelve fabulous projects that combine quilting and embroidery. Patterns for quilts and embroidery designs are included on a free CD-ROM.

Softcover • 8¼ x 10⅞ • 144 pages
75 color photos, 75 illus.

Item# MEQ • $27.99

Machine Embroidery Room by Room
30+ Home Dècor Projects
by Carol Zentgraf

Tackle a small-scale home makeover with themes and three design groupings for eight unique rooms, featured in 30+ projects and demonstrated in more than 200+ color photos and illustrations.

Softcover • 8¼ x 10⅞ • 128 pages
200+ color photos and illus.

Item# MEHD • $29.99

Machine Embroidery With Confidence
A Beginner's Guide
by Nancy Zieman

Nancy Zieman explains the basics of machine embroidery including what tools to use, how to organize the embroidery area, types of machines, designs, templating/positioning, software, stabilizers, troubleshooting and finishing touches.

Softcover • 8¼ x 10⅞ • 128 pages
100 color photos

Item# CFEM • $21.99

Machine Embroidery on Paper
by Annette Gentry Bailey

This exciting reference takes machine embroidery into paper crafts with 30+ cool embroidered projects including cards, frames, boxes and sachets. Features 20 original embroidery designs on an enclosed CD-ROM.

Softcover • 8¼ x 10⅞ • 48 pages
115+ color photos & illus.
Item# MEPP • $22.99

Embroidery Machine Essentials: Fleece Techniques
Jeanine Twigg's Companion Project Series #2
by Nancy Cornwell

This second Companion Project Series book covering the "how-to" secrets for machine embroidery success combines fleece and embroidery in 20 easy-to-stitch projects using the book and CD combination

Softcover • 8¼ x 10⅞ • 48 pages
color throughout
Item# EMSF • $19.95

Machine Embroidery Wild & Wacky
Stitch on Any and Every Surface
by Linda Griepentrog and Rebecca Kemp Brent

Go beyond machine embroidery basics using unique bases such as wood and canvas, and techniques including embossing and painting, and apply to 28 projects featured on bonus CD.

Softcover • 8¼ x 10⅞ • 128 pages
225 color photos and illus.

Item# MEWA • $29.99